Degrading the Grading Myths:
A Primer of Alternatives to Grades and Marks

Sidney B. Simon and James A. Bellanca, Editors
Foreword by Philip L. Hosford

William J. Bailey

James A. Bellanca

Keith V. Burba

Arthur W. Combs

Richard L. Curwin

Patrick J. DeMarte

Patrick J. Dowling

Francis B. Evans

Lois Borland Hart

Donald D. Holt

Howard Kirschenbaum

Rodney W. Napier

Sandra Folzer Napier

Sidney B. Simon

James B. Van Hoven

Prepared in Cooperation
with the National Center
for Grading/Learning Alternatives

Association for Supervision and Curriculum Development
1701 K Street, N.W.
Suite 1100
Washington, D.C. 20006

Stock Number: 611-76082

Final editing of the manuscript and publication of this booklet were the
responsibility of Robert R. Leeper, Associate Director and Editor, ASCD
publications. Technical production was handled by Carol Feld, Elsa Angell,
Polly Larson, and Teola T. Jones, with Nancy Olson as production manager.

Library of Congress Catalog Card Number: 76-20413

Contents

Part III / Some Alternatives That Work

Part IV / Changing the System

Foreword

THIS IS THE kind of book one expects from ASCD. It addresses a serious problem—that of grading—in keeping with the long-term concerns of curriculum leaders throughout the land. In it, we learn from psychology, research, case studies, philosophy, good writing, and enjoyable reading.

For years I have believed that problems generated by the formal grading of learners will never go away—regardless of who does the grading or how it is done. But a careful reading of this "primer" might lessen the magnitude of those problems. Here, successful grading alternatives are presented for use in elementary and secondary classrooms, and in universities. Principals, supervisors, and curriculum leaders will find in the models presented much of the help they need to cause and control change in grading policies and practices.

The book has a startling integrity. Each chapter adds to that integrity, and yet, stands alone in value to the reader. The common interests, concerns, and efforts of those involved in curriculum development, supervision, and instruction are neatly woven throughout all four parts of the book.

The volume is introduced by Sid Simon's discussion of the "Wad-Ja-Get?" syndrome—society's obsession with grades—and where it has led. Simon also explains each author's strong identification with the grading issue, and presents seven major questions that the authors, in this book, attempt to answer. His overview provides a helpful perspective for considering all the material to follow.

Part I presents the problem, beginning with Art Combs' "stage-setting" comments about the nature of learning and his discussion of four criteria for determining procedures in grading. Later in this section,

Sid Simon's delightful writing leads us to rediscover the many ingenious methods of cheating that students use in grade-getting—methods that might never have been invented had no grading system ever been devised. Enjoyable reading with a strong message!

Part II provides a quick review of what research has had to say on the subject of grading and presents us with valuable references. The pros and cons of several alternative grading/evaluating schemes are also reviewed. Although most of the research presented confirms the fact that grading is, indeed, a problem, much attention is given to typical humanistic concerns about that problem.

Five successful alternative (non-common) grading procedures are presented in Part III. These case studies range from a personal report about procedures in a college classroom, to notes on a computerized grading system, to a faculty-developed evaluation plan for an entire school district.

Methods of changing the grading system are presented in Part IV, and, with a parting shot, four myths of grading are dropped to their appropriate levels of validity.

I introduce this book to its professional audience with equal portions of pride and enthusiasm. The authors and editors are to be commended for their contributions. I predict the impact of this book will be noted by educational historians because of the difference it will make in the classrooms, school districts, and colleges of our country.

And, after all—that is what ASCD is all about!

PHILIP L. HOSFORD, *President 1976-77*
Association for Supervision and
Curriculum Development

An Overview

No LEVEL OF education is free from it; no teacher or student can hide from it. The cry of "Wad-Ja-Get?" is all around us.

The "Wad-Ja-Get?" refrain that accompanies the grading system in American education is as pervasive as our questions about higher taxes, increased smog, and rising inflation. Students, from kindergarten through graduate school, feel the ache of the "Wad-Ja-Get?" syndrome; most know that it dominates more of their learning than they would ever care to admit. Teachers likewise deal with the grading problem, from the first day they enter a classroom until the moment they file their last record book and retire. School administrators spend countless hours on "Wad-Ja-Get?" as well; they grapple with parents—who have already grappled with their children's teachers—about the "fairness" and "rightness" of grades.

Wherever teaching and learning go on, grades are a grim reality for most people; that much is clear. But beyond the reality is an enormous amount of confusion and arguing about grading, a phenomenon that—by touching the lives of almost every human being—has an impact incredibly wide and deep. To ignore the complexity of the grading issue is to live in a fantasy world where houses are made of gingerbread, the stork delivers babies, and failure has no effect on a person's life.

The essays that have been collected in this book contain some of the best and freshest ideas about how we assess student performance through the phenomenon we call grading, marking, evaluating, and reporting. Although this collection is not completely unbiased, the contributing authors have made a serious effort to consider all facets of the grading issue. While most of them argue for broad grading reform,

1

specific changes, or an end to the emotional damage inflicted on many students in the name of grading and marking, none attacks the system in an illogical or polemical way.

Experiencing the Effects of Grading

The teachers and administrators who share their experiences and findings in this book have sweated for years under the time deadlines and other pressures that grades present. Many have watched teary-eyed students beg and plead for a B-plus to be recorded as an A-minus in order to escape being "grounded" or barred by their parents from attending the junior prom. The authors know how such students must feel when they go home and are met at the door with the cry, "Wad-Ja-Get?"

Most of the authors have also seen another type of student—the cold, canny, crafty apple-polisher who moves sleekly through the classroom. Clever and carefully conniving, such students will spout Toynbee-isms if they sense their teachers like Toynbee, then change ground (without losing a step) should they discover that Buber, not Toynbee, is the actual favorite. Their shifts, like those of the chameleon, are miraculous and instantaneous.

Several of the writers have caught a student of theirs cheating and have been overwhelmed by the agonizing thought that they, through grades, might be cutting off that student's chance at a successful future. It is disheartening to have seen a student *so desperate* that his or her moral system, admirable in every other way, has crumbled under the pressure to get a good grade. It is even worse to have had students who choose to jump from dormitory windows rather than face transcripts that show them to be on the lower end of the bell-shaped curve.

Tackling Some of the Questions

Those who think grades are a minor problem just haven't been looking very hard at what is happening. Grades impinge upon and shape more teaching-learning situations than most people will ever imagine, unless they start looking at the problem with the emotional intensity and deep concern that the authors of this volume possess.

In this collection of essays, some fine and humanistic minds tackle many of the hard questions we all wrestle with in education. This is a practical book that provides the rich background anyone needs who wishes to tackle the grading issue. It also contains research information that does what information should do: inform our values. Perhaps most importantly, it includes two vitally useful sections on *alternatives that work* and *changing the system.*

The effort here has been to cast some light on the following essential and frequently asked questions—all of which surround the grading and marking issue.

1. Without the incentive to get good grades, how can students be motivated to learn? (Among the contributors who try to answer this question are Combs, Bailey, Holt, and Simon.)

2. Aren't grades necessary for college admissions? (See the chapter by Evans on research, as well as the chapter by Bellanca and Kirschenbaum on grading alternatives.)

3. Don't grades at least ensure that students will achieve minimum competencies? (Read the views of Combs and Evans, plus the narrative piece by Kirschenbaum, Simon, and Napier.)

4. Aren't grades the best predictors of later student success? (Actually, they are quite crude predictors. See almost any of the essays to dispel this myth.)

5. If teachers spend enough time and are extremely careful in assigning grades, can't grading be an accurate and objective measure of student performance? (See the separate analyses of Holt, Dowling, and Simon.)

6. People are naturally competitive, so what else can teachers do except give them what they want: grades? (See the comments of Curwin and DeMarte about this, as well as those of Hart and Simon.)

7. There aren't any viable alternatives to grades and marks, are there? (Review the entire section on alternatives, plus the section on changing the system.)

Defining Our Purposes

Those who have contributed to this book feel a deep sense of satisfaction in seeing it come to life. It will serve a worthwhile purpose if it does nothing more than cause some complacent people to question what has happened to millions of learners and their teachers under the guise of allegedly "objective" grading and marking.

The major purpose of the book is, however, to show that there *are* alternatives to the conventional grading system. It is absurd to perpetuate any system simply because it exists, as Shirley Jackson points out so well in her powerful short story, "The Lottery." [1] Jackson's characters are villagers who meet once a year to pick, by lottery, someone they will stone to death. They do not seem to consider the inhumanity of the tradition they have followed, unquestioningly, for as long as they can remember. After all, there has *always* been a lottery. Unfortunately, many of us are like the villagers Jackson describes; we defend the grading system because it exists, and because we know nothing else.

The writers who present their ideas in this book have lived too many years as learners, teachers, administrators, and/or parents not to feel more than casually what grades have meant and what grades—as a force impinging either positively or negatively on our lives—have caused us to do and to become. Because we have felt acutely the agony of what grades have done and can continue to do, we have a sincere commitment to search for more life-giving alternatives that will bring a greater degree of sanity to the marking and grading "game" than now exists.

Over 50 years ago, researchers Starch and Elliott performed "mind-blowing" experiments whose results refuted the reliability of grades. In the past 50-plus years, millions of students have been systematically wounded by the grading and marking system. It is time to change that system, and this book is an urgent call to change. The authors and editors are proud that the Association for Supervision and Curriculum Development has answered the call, and will be making this book available to educational leaders who have the ability to determine whether the existing grading system will be perpetuated, or whether substantial change will be effected.

Fifty years is a long time to stand still. Let's get moving.

SIDNEY B. SIMON
June 1976

---

[1] Shirley Jackson. "The Lottery." In: *The Lottery: Adventures of the Daemon Lover.* New York: Avon Books, 1960.

Part I

The Issues: To Grade or To Learn?

"So, what's wrong with grades? I received school grades and I survived. Why spoil all these kids?"—*a parent*

"Life is competitive. Grades teach survival skills."—*a teacher*

"Grades tell me where I stand."—*a student*

"Grades are very efficient."—*a registrar*

THE ISSUES THAT surround grading reform are complex and confusing. Advocates of grades and marks sound like these quotes. In addition to arguing for competitive schools, exact expectations, efficient records, and learning by pain, they also argue the importance of grades to college entrance, jobs, and the nature of motivation.

On the opposite side are the advocates of reform. Some see grading reform as a means to improve traditional learning; others see it as an end in itself. In both cases reformists argue about improving self-concept and ending cheating, the negative effects of competition, the damage caused by failure, and the other deleterious consequences of grading.

In this section, the authors examine the grading issues from a humanistic view. None favors the retention of traditional grades because they all start with the premise that a child's growth and learning will be enriched by support and help; in most cases, grades are perceived in these articles as restrictive and punitive.

What We Know About Learning and Criteria for Practice*

Arthur W. Combs

WHATEVER WE DO with the problem of grading will be a function of the beliefs we hold about the nature of motivation and learning. For a long time our educational system has been predicating many of its operations on inadequate interpretations of these concepts. We have conceived of the problems of motivation and learning using the S-R construct that most of us cut our teeth on. In this view motivation is seen as manipulation of the stimulus by an outsider, and learning is seen as change in behavior usually accomplished by manipulating the stimulus and/or controlling the response through management techniques. Education has lived in the grip of these conceptions for years. Currently we are beginning to understand the problems of motivation and learning in a different way.

As a consequence of humanistic approaches to psychological thought, we are beginning to understand the problem of learning in more holistic terms as a problem in the discovery of personal meaning. The basic problem can be stated simply as follows: *Any information will have an effect upon the behavior of an individual only to the degree that he or she has discovered the personal meaning of that information for himself or herself.*

This principle has vast implications for all aspects of education. It means that learning happens inside people; it is a subjective experience. The behavior we observe is only a symptom of that which is going on within the individual. An educational system exclusively preoccupied

* The above article is adapted from a speech made by the author at the First National Conference on Grading Alternatives, Cleveland, Ohio, October, 1972.

6

with behavior and behavioral change is a system dealing only with symptoms, and is likely to be no more effective than the doctor who only treats symptoms without ever dealing with their causes.

It is necessary to understand that all learning is affective and that affect must be understood in terms of relevance. Feeling or affect increases in direct proportion to the individual's perception of the importance of any particular event to the self. Concepts which are not seen as having a bearing on self can be dealt with objectively, without feeling. Events having to do with one's basic self, however, are another matter; they are met with feeling. Education must be affective or there will be none at all.

If learning is understood as the personal discovery of meaning, then motivation becomes an internal matter having to do with people's beliefs, attitudes, feelings, values, hopes, desires, and the like. Whatever happens in the classroom must be understood in these terms.

The dynamics of what goes on in the classroom can only be adequately comprehended in terms of both the teacher's purposes, what he or she is trying to do on the one hand, and the child's perceptions of what seems to be occurring on the other. How the activities of the classroom look to an outside observer of the process is likely to be very largely irrelevant and can actually lead to totally wrong conclusions about what is going on there. What happens is a function of the perceptions of teachers and students.

This new conception of learning emphasizes the absolutely crucial character of the student's self-concept. We now understand that an individual's self-concept determines his or her behavior in almost everything that person does. It also affects intelligence, for people who believe they are *able* will try, while those who believe they are *unable* will not. Self-concept also plays a highly important role in the goals of self-actualization and in the extent to which an individual is likely to achieve a high degree of health and effectiveness. The self-concept, however, is learned from the feedback we get from the people who surround us in the processes of our growing up and living. Positive views of self are characteristic of healthy individuals while negative views of self are characteristic of the sick and the neurotic. Thus, self-actualization becomes a problem in the fulfillment or deprivation of self, and effective learning—as a problem in self-discovery—must somehow lead to positive views of self.

If learning is a problem in personal discovery its achievement is brought about through effective problem solving. This means that classrooms must challenge students without threatening them. When people feel threatened they are turned off. Threat has the effect of narrowing perception and forcing self-defense, neither of which is conducive to the goals of education. Challenge, on the other hand, encourages and facilitates the processes of learning. People feel challenged when they are confronted with problems that interest them and that they believe they have a chance of mastering. Alternatively, people feel threatened when they are confronted with problems they do not feel adequate to handle. Whether persons feel challenged or threatened by whatever goes on in the classroom, however, is not a function of how it seems to outsiders but of how it seems to participants.

Whatever is done in the name of education must deal with four criteria and the problem of grading is no exception:

1. *Are the objectives sought by whatever is done the truly important ones?* At the present time we are going all out for behavioral objectives and accountability; the net result of all this is that frequently we are letting our objectives be determined by default. We measure what we know how to measure rather than what we need to measure and, as a consequence, our objectives frequently deal only with the simplest, most primitive aspects of the problem. The real sickness of American education today is its irrelevance and dehumanization. We cannot afford to concentrate our evaluative devices upon less than the most important aspects of education. After all, we can get along better with a bad reader in our society than with a bigot. It is important to recognize that systems approaches are a means to guarantee arrival at our objectives. Applied to the wrong objectives they will only guarantee that our errors are colossal!

2. *Is the device used the best way of achieving the objectives we have decided upon?* Here we must ask whether the techniques we are using to achieve the objectives we have determined will truly measure the goals we seek. We know that intelligence is correlated with foot size, but few of us would utilize the size of a person's foot as an adequate measure of intelligence. The importance of the adequacy of the sample is a fundamental principle in research. It ought not be overlooked in determining the objectives of education.

3. *What is the effect on the teacher?* Such effects on the user are often ignored in the introduction of techniques to the education process. Nevertheless, effects are inevitable and whatever we do in the way of assessment of human beings necessarily controls attention, focuses behavior, and determines the goals that teachers seek. These effects must certainly be considered in whatever we do in applying any method of assessment.

4. *Finally, the effects on the student must be considered in whatever we do in assessing classroom operations.* This means we must also be concerned about side effects. Members of the medical profession are very careful to check out the side effects of any new drug they introduce but, in education, we often ignore side effects. It is necessary to remember that the student brings his self-concept to class with him and that whatever happens in the classroom is affecting his self-concept as well as the concepts he acquires with respect to a body of knowledge. These effects on the self-concept cannot be ignored because they are inconvenient to the learning process. The laws of learning cannot be set aside; they must be dealt with lest we "lose on the bananas what we made on the oranges."

If learning and motivation are to be seen in the humanistic ways in which we now begin to understand them, then all of us must actively check ourselves and our classroom procedures, including the problems of grading and assessment. We must search out the barriers to personal discovery wherever they exist and remove them from the path of the student. At the same time, all of us must learn to value problem solving and personal discovery in the light of our new conceptions of learning. We should actively seek to stimulate and encourage student involvement, commitment, and personal discovery in every way we can, in whatever areas of human growth for which we are responsible.

An Experience with Failure

Donald D. Holt

RECENTLY I TAUGHT a foundations course in education at Portland State University. I began to notice that the subject under discussion—the concept of failure and its effects on students—was not having the impact that I had hoped it would. The books we were reading (*The Professional Education of Teachers* [1] and *In Defense of Youth* [2]) had stimulated some discussion, but what could not be communicated were the *feelings* that I think accompany failure—the emotional impact that failure has on so many students.

My own thinking and experience have led me to believe that too few teachers have given attention to the effects of failing their students. Teachers, by the very requirements of their profession, are men and women who have had very few, if any, unsuccessful experiences in schools. Consequently, the diminution of self that often accompanies failure, and the expanding repercussions of failure on all dimensions of a student's life are feelings and consequences quite foreign to most teachers.

As a result of the class discussion about failure, I decided to engineer a small negative experience for my students. I hoped it would produce

[1] Arthur W. Combs. *The Professional Education of Teachers.* Boston, Massachusetts: Allyn and Bacon, Inc., 1974.

[2] Earl C. Kelley. *In Defense of Youth.* Englewood Cliffs, New Jersey: Prentice-Hall, Inc., 1962.

in them the complete awareness I view as a necessary condition for learning. (I call what took place an "experience" only because I can think of no other term to describe it.)

My purpose in creating an atmosphere of failure was to show my students, by object lesson, that if real learning is to occur, one critical element must be present: *personal meaning*. Ultimately, it is personal meaning—the significance of information to an individual—that allows "the facts" he or she learns to take on dimensions far beyond those of most traditional classroom experiences.

In order to make the learning experience as meaningful as possible, I had to establish the criteria I feel are usually present when a student fails. Since there is seldom any valuable communication between "teacher" and student during a failure experience, I held no office hours during which students could talk with me. I also reduced the classroom verbal pattern to lecture only. I allowed no one to interrupt me during a lecture and I timed each lecture to run exactly 40 minutes.

There is also, I feel, an excessive emphasis on measurement during a failure experience since the quality and quantity of what is learned is determined by testing students. From this, teachers determine whether students have met course standards. In a failure experience they don't, and the teachers can prove it! So I gave my classes a ten-minute test each day at the beginning of the period on the reading matter for the week. The tests, of course, were very challenging, as was the curve I established prior to each test.

During a failure experience you will also find that a teacher reminds students they are doing poorly by writing negative comments on paper (in red pencil) and by holding the circled red F's over their heads as a measure of their ineptness. Naturally, I did both.

I had originally planned that the experience would last for one week; it never got that far. By Thursday, my twelve o'clock section revolted. They were led by a bright, articulate young woman who refused to continue in an environment in which she was "nothing more than a test, a grade, and a listener." She refused to take the Thursday morning examination and rose in anger to ask her classmates if they wished to continue in the class. Those who did not, she encouraged to join her in an assault on the Dean's office to see if they could get me fired, lynched, or both. At this point I stopped the experience for the twelve o'clock section.

My other two classes were less overtly rebellious by Thursday, but they had become unbearable to live with. They responded with disdain to the tests, whispered to their neighbors, looked out the windows while I lectured, or read some important material for their next classes.

Some just cut the class or came very close to it. ("I considered being a class dropout on Thursday. . . ." "I considered not even coming to class.") Some, of course, were there only in body. ("I just couldn't sit still—kept counting the minutes." "I thought of skipping some classes and even though I went, I found myself not listening. . . .") How often do teachers see their students acting the same way, but refuse to consider that their teaching practices may be contributing to these actions and feelings?

In college a student can leave the cold, indifferent instructor, who appears to regard him or her as something less than a human being, and seek out one who does not. Elementary and secondary students often are trapped by regulations that will not allow class changes once the school year has begun. This combination of entrapment and insensitivity can destroy in children any hope of making school a place where they can be successful.

There are, of course, those few brave souls who will complain to their parents or counselors, or even escape from it all by dropping out. But most, rather than appear different or questionable, seek solace in their classmates—searching for those with similar feelings for or reactions to teachers who, they are convinced, do not care for them. Many of my students did the same thing. ("I was more comfortable knowing I was not alone." "If I hadn't become aware that others were doing as poorly as I, then the effects would have been more potent.")

Another damaging effect of the failure experience was the discouragement it produced in many students. ("I felt that maybe I was too dumb to even try to stay in school." "I quit carrying too many courses.") It was alarming to see how shaky the self-confidence became in my class of intelligent, prospective teachers. If it takes only this to damage successful high school graduates ("I felt dumb."), what must happen to young minds when they first meet this kind of experience? Are they ever really the same again?

Failure can also build in students strong resentment toward what threatens them. Their vision will narrow and in many cases it will be the teacher against whom students harbor the greatest feelings of distrust and anger. ("I didn't know whether to poke you in the nose, quit school and go back to my old job, or what." ". . . disliked you intensely.") If the failure experience is repeated enough, such feelings can extend to an entire educational institution. This is so often the case with failing students or dropouts; their disappointment in themselves and the school is so great that they can only think of fleeing from or destroying the causes of their discomfort. Many of the students in my classes began to exhibit the first twinges of this destructive force. On Friday, at the conclusion of the experience their relief was so apparent, it was as if they had been freed to return to that which was again normal and rewarding.

Most of the circumstances I created were overdone to the point of distortion. To be more significant, a failure experience should be generated over a much longer period of time, with greater subtlety and deception. My attempts were at least conscious: I wanted my students to experience failure. The tragedy is that all too often teachers do not want failure to be the result of their effort, but they have no control over what previous failure may have already instilled in the child or what threats of failure may ultimately do to the student.

If the experience described had any value, my hope is that it gave each student a brief glimpse of what insensitive, subject-centered teaching can do to those attempting to learn. If these future teachers can remember the experience long enough to see that it never happens with their own students, then perhaps something was accomplished. They will, of course, by the nature of public education, have to fail some students. If they think a bit about what their students will feel, however, they may try harder to create an environment in which failure does not have to be the outcome.

Some students expressed the feelings that I hoped they would. ("I never realized how powerful the tongue and pen can be and how damaging . . . to a student." "I learned a lesson I will never forget—how it feels to fail.") Perhaps they realize now that failure can destroy. If they understand this much, I did a bit of teaching.

Making Classroom Competition Positive: A Facilitating Model*

Richard L. Curwin and Patrick J. DeMarte

MR. BARTON GAVE his class a reading test to determine group placement for the remainder of the year. Although the students did not understand how the tests were to be used, they did learn through rumor, that the tests were very important and would tell Mr. Barton how smart they were. Many students tried to read answers from their neighbors' papers.

Ms. Lyons runs an open classroom. She allows students to select social studies objectives and learning activities from a source bank. The students are required to do only what they choose at the beginning of each week. Ms. Lyons has placed a chart at the front of the room listing every student's name along with the objectives selected and achieved on a day-to-day basis. The five students who have completed the most objectives at the end of every week receive special privileges.

Competitive activities like these are commonplace in classrooms across the country. Close examination of similar instances might reveal cheating, compromised values, and threats to self-concept.

Contemporary educators are taking a long, hard look at the competitiveness of learning and are coming up with two contradictory sets of conclusions. Proponents of competition in education extol its virtue:

* The above article first appeared under the title, "Competition Can Be Positive," in *Scholastic Teacher*, Teachers Edition, April 10, 1975. It is reprinted with permission from *Scholastic Teacher*, © 1975 by Scholastic Magazines, Inc.

training for the cutthroat, real-life world waiting in the wings. Opponents claim that all competition is harmful and must be eliminated from the school environment if the child is to survive psychologically.

It is unfortunate that the issue of competition is considered in "either/or" terms, because such a restrictive view provides an inaccurate picture of how competition works, and worse, such a view leaves the teacher confused, and without realistic, viable options for everyday classroom situations. Few classrooms are void of competition, just as few classrooms have no cooperation.

There is a third alternative for understanding competition and how it relates to learning. It is a model that can be readily applied to real classroom situations so that teachers can facilitate learning through healthy competitions that do not destroy self-concepts or encourage "me first" attitudes. The model contains three independent factors common to all competition: conditions of entry; emphasis; and control. These factors are used to define competitive situations so that the effects of any competition may be determined. These three factors, as well as competition as a whole, are viewed in this model as a continuum and not exclusively in "either/or" terms.

Conditions of Entry

Is participation in the competition voluntary or involuntary? Voluntary participation means that participants have a free choice in the decision to compete. Use of overt and subtle pressures to influence a person's decision to partake in the competition is not acceptable. Some classroom examples are:

• Students may choose instructional groups on the basis of interest rather than be placed in predetermined ability groups in which a norm of behavior is expected;
• Students may choose from a wide variety of learning activities;
• No student is ever pressured to participate in a particular classroom activity. The student's right to pass is accepted without question.

Involuntary entry, on the other hand, includes those situations in which, knowingly or unknowingly, a person is forced or coerced to participate. Some examples are:

• All students take the same exam at the same time;
• Everyone must participate in the same events or activities;
• Students are grouped by ability for instructional purposes.

The more freedom a student has in choosing to compete, the more likely the competition will be in his or her best interest. Each student is the best judge of whether to enter a competition. The removal of the threat or coercion to compete helps students choose the competitions that have personal meaning for them.

Emphasis

Is the competition primarily geared toward means or ends? Means-centered situations are characterized by an emphasis on the process involved in the competition; winning or losing is not as important as the learning that occurs. Means-centered competition is further exemplified by the existence of internal rewards, such as learning for learning's sake, playing for the enjoyment of the game, striving to increase ability or achieve a personal goal. Some classroom examples are:

• No external rewards or punishments are granted for academic effort (excludes using letter and numerical grades, passing out test papers according to marks earned, and failing students);
• Noncomparative feedback is provided for all student work;
• Students are allowed to progress at their own rates.

Ends-centered competition is characterized by emphasis on results in terms of winning or losing, with rewards only for those who win; losers are considered failures. In ends-centered competition, rewards are classified as external, whereas, in means-centered competition rewards are primarily internal. Examples of ends-centered competition are:

• Report cards are sent home with letter or numerical grades;
• Achievement charts are displayed in the classroom;
• Praise and criticism are used to coerce students into achieving teacher-determined outcomes.

Ends-centered competition is costly to winners and losers alike. Advocates of competition claim that it can result in pride, teamwork, sacrifice—all fundamental skills necessary for success; aspiration for greater achievement levels; and the ability to face defeat with a healthy attitude. By placing stress on the ends, however, we destroy the potential of all these benefits and create a climate which encourages cheating, cutting corners, and general distrust. The result is unhealthy attitudes which actually hinder learning and the personal growth of our students.

Control

Is the responsibility for enforcing rules of the competition the role of an external or internal agent? Situations involving internal responsibility require that the participating individuals have decision-making responsibility and that they use it with objectivity and fairness. Some classroom examples are:

• Students and teacher share the responsibility for evaluating work;
• In classroom games, each player is responsible for maintaining the rules.

To be effective, an external judgment system demands that those persons with decision-making responsibility must be objective and must possess the knowledge and skills to make fair judgments. Some examples are:

• Only the teacher's criteria are used in evaluating student work (for example, the teacher gives an exam, grades it, and returns it);
• The responsibility for preventing and policing cheating is exclusively the teacher's;
• In classroom games, the teacher always states and enforces the rules.

Delegating responsibility to others for enforcing rules (through an external judgment system) promotes moral irresponsibility, especially in learning situations. Students adopt the attitude, "It's okay to do something wrong as long as I don't get caught." They need a chance to develop moral integrity, and the first step is accepting the responsibility for enforcing the rules that apply to their own behavior. (See Table 1.)

		Conditions of Entry	
		Voluntary	Involuntary
	MEANS— Internal	VMI *	IMI
Emphasis and Control	MEANS— External	VME	IME
	ENDS— Internal	VEI	IEI
	ENDS— External	VEE	IEE

* VMI is an abbreviation which represents a competitive situation where participation is voluntary, means are emphasized, and control is internal. All other characterizations follow this pattern.

Table 1. Operational Definitions of Competitive Situations

We find that competitive situations characterized by Voluntary Entry, Means Emphasis, and Internal Control (VMI) are in the best interests of students, particularly as such situations relate to self-concept. VMI situations are nonthreatening and help students to reach their full potential. On the other hand, competitive situations characterized by Involuntary Entry, Ends Emphasis, and External Control (IEE) are typically detrimental to students. Both VMI and IEE are extreme conditions; most competition lies somewhere between the two. However, the closer the situation to the condition VMI, the better the competition is for the students.

The classroom, as the basic unit for education in our society, provides numerous sources of competition, many subtle and difficult for the average teacher to detect. Potential sources of competition in the classroom include the obvious examples of tracking; earning special privileges and responsibilities (being a corridor marshal or doing errands); attaining social, academic, or leadership status; achieving popularity (with students and teacher); maintaining the teacher's attention; and gaining recognition through sports and educational games. The clearest and most prominent area of competition in the classroom is grading.

Comparative grading is clearly an example of IEE competition since students have no choice of how or if they are to be graded. Also, grades, by their very nature, stress ends not means. Grades encourage students to concentrate on rewards (or punishments) rather than on learning. The responsibility of enforcing the grading system rests solely with the teacher. The pressure put on students to succeed causes cheating, dropping out (physically, as well as intellectually and emotionally), and undue stress for students and teachers alike.

Many systems of assessing student progress are available. Those in which at least one of the VMI criteria applies could have positive effects on students' self-concepts and their attitudes toward school.

The teacher can change a competitive classroom situation into a VMI situation. The first step is to identify different areas of competition that exist in individual classrooms. The previously suggested list represents possible sources of competition, yet each classroom has its own unique characteristics. Each teacher must draw up a specific list for his or her own situation. The teacher can then apply the criteria to each competition discerned, determine its nature, and assess its relative effects on the students involved. With the help of students and colleagues (including administrators), a teacher can then determine ways to derive maximum benefits from the competitions.

It is predominantly up to the teacher to ensure that competitions are positive experiences for students. By choosing competitive structures that are characterized by VMI, and by working with students so that they can recognize and choose VMI situations themselves, the teacher can, in effect, reap many of the rewards of competition while avoiding most of the pitfalls.

Who Ever Cheats To Learn?

Sidney B. Simon

THE BIG THING about cheating that we all should remember is that no one—man, woman, or child—ever cheats to learn. Cheating gains us neither information, nor knowledge, nor least of all, wisdom.

Still, students, through the ages, have cheated. They have cheated to avoid punishment, cheated to maintain academic standing, cheated to "up themselves" on the establishment's staircase, and cheated to gain status.

Cheating is a direct outcome of an overly competitive grading and marking system. The more pressure generated in a given classroom or school system, the more abundant the cheating will be. With the removal of grades and marks, cheating disappears and students begin to help one another learn what they have to learn. Cheating is always abundant when rewards are in short supply. A classroom in which cheating flourishes is like a family without enough love to go around. A child in such a family will get another in trouble to gain love by default. Trouble is a strange way to buy love; cheating is an even stranger way to gain rewards.

Cheaters become more and more creative in their desperate scramble to reach a higher rung on the ladder of success. A catalog of cheating methods could go on endlessly. Consider these favorites:

Cheating on True and False: Anyone who has been a student must be familiar with methods of cheating on true and false questions. (Is there an implication that teachers were never students if they don't know them?) In most student worlds, there is a basic way to pass back and

20

forth the true-false answer. Two fingers up on the right hand, three up on the left = question #23. The cooperative answer (Who ever said pressure was the antithesis of cooperation?) is flashed back with a one-finger-on-the-nose. Jot down true. If you get two-fingers-on-the-nose, the answer to good old #23 is false. A finger up the nose signals that you should rely on self-help because this test is graded on a curve and the name of the game is survival-of-the-least-helpful.

Cheating on a Multiple Choice Question: This is a more sophisti-cated version of fingers-on-the-nose. Given the fact that there are usually four choices on a multiple choice question, you could probably go with one-, two-, three-, or four-fingers-on-the-nose. But too many fingers crowd the nose, so cultured cheaters have devised the "foot position" to handle multiple choices. Use your left foot for A and B choices, and your right foot for C and D. Point your left foot to the far left for choice A and to the far right for choice B. Use the same subtle twists with your right foot for choices C or D. Tactful, yes. And very successful.

The Crib Sheet: Memorizing information is a proverbial "drag" for students. But teachers love to be drags. Thus students must learn creativity by devising crib sheets to avoid memorizing the tons of infor-mation which they and the teachers know will never be used again. (For example, name the four Stuart kings or give the formula for measuring a flagpole's height at 10 A.M., 10 degrees north of the equator, assuming you are living in Maine, on June 10, 1010 B.C.)

The simplest method I have heard described is to tape 4″ x 6″ crib cards to the legs. Another involves answers painfully sketched on finger-nails or inked on Necco wafers. (What proctor would deny a student sustenance in the midst of final exam week!) The most creative crib I have seen is a watch device. The student had rigged his wrist watch with a roll of rice paper aptly inscribed with all the chemistry formulas he needed. Fiddle with the watch and the scroll of answers unfurls undetected.

But the most ingenious story of all tells about the young man who appeared at his final exam with his head swathed in bandages. Only two beady eyes showed. He told his professor how much the course meant—how he dragged himself from his hospital bed just for the exam. The professor was so touched, he failed to realize that inside the bandage was a transistorized radio ready to relay. When stumped with a question, the student would mumble outloud, "Oh, why can't I remember those darn seven products of Argentina?" Lo and behold, over the two-way radio came the voice of a loyal fraternity brother: "Wool, leather . . ."

As absurd as these instances seem, there are many other examples each of us could share. There is no record of how many times the same term papers are turned in to the same departments, or even to the same professors. No tally exists of the dollars paid to ghost writers for papers short and long, and even for doctoral dissertations. No matter how relentless professors and teachers are in the never ceasing battle against plagiarism, term papers are glued together with other people's words. Where grades mean medical school, the bar, professional life or death, the stakes are too high for honesty and learning. From bibliographies of unread books to copied Spanish homework, cheating means survival.

When will teachers discover that without a grading system, there is no cheating? We all recognize that, without grades, certain teachers would leave the classroom, certain subjects would disappear from curricula, and useless memorization would die a natural death. All would go, as they should, into the valley of the forgotten.

Unfortunately, until the college-entrance-grad-school-hysteria takes on a semblance of reason, the grading rat race, the "paper chase," will continue. Students molded by grade point average (GPA), rank in class (RIC), and other destructive symbols will set ethics aside and cheat their way into the golden mean.

Grading and Young Children

Sandra Folzer Napier

DO YOU CONSIDER yourself fairly smart or not? And when did you first perceive yourself in this way? Chances are good that your vital self-concept germinated early in your school career. Possibly it was at the onset of your tortuous grading history. It is likely that some innocent teacher was simply performing his or her duty by giving you a grade of some sort. He or she did not intend to assign you to lifelong membership in the smart, the dumb, or the just plain-old-average group. But there you are, twenty years later.

Even if you've graduated to a higher status group, even if you now believe you're fairly intelligent, do some doubts still creep in? You could have become just a hard worker; underneath, you still may be the mediocre student someone once said you were. How difficult it is to free oneself from those early images. If you're one of the more fortunate achievers, you see yourself positively, and you may not understand what all the fuss is about. How would you feel—can you attempt to imagine—what it would be like if you were called "dumb"? The word might be a tag you would try to shed throughout your lifetime, or a condemnation you might come to accept. You might. After all, "they" know more than you do. Those teachers are the experts.

Others Contribute to Self-Concept

Certainly there is much more to a person's self-concept than level of intelligence. Concerns about social and physical attractiveness, skills,

23

preferences, perceptions: All of these and more contribute to the images and ideas we have of ourselves. We form composite pictures of ourselves—amassed from the experiences surrounding us at home, in playgrounds, on neighbors' porches, as well as in schools. Since more than 50 percent of a child's waking hours are spent in school, he or she cannot be spared the constant exposure to the reactions of others, a mirror in which we all view ourselves.

·As much as we would like to develop relatively free from the confines of the perceptions of others, it is difficult; perhaps it is even impossible. Nearly all persons are affected in some way by how others see them. We certainly do not choose this fate; it simply happens. Children are no exception. They begin life with a clear slate. If left alone in the wilderness to be raised by wolves, they may never have to question their intelligence or their sociability. They may never lose the naturalness spoken of by Rousseau. However, society exacts a toll for the security it provides: We are classified, formed, and then fitted to the existing system. Comparison and, too often, competition result. Who we *are* sometimes becomes dependent on who others are as well. Someone always stands to lose.

Impact of Grades

Understanding the possible injury grading might inflict on anyone, but especially a vulnerable child, the educator might investigate the differences between grading and evaluation. The latter is definitely essential to any educational process; the former is not. Grading implies a limiting process through which the individual is forced into some artificial category for the sake of efficiency. Evaluation, on the other hand, implies a discovery, an application of some value to a particular behavior. It suggests a specific assessment, not a long-range classification. The words of some very capable fourth graders emphasize the impact of grades on young children:

If I got bad grades, I'd think I was stupid . . . didn't know anything.

Once I remember going home [with bad grades] and screaming and jumping on my bed. I wanted to tell my mom I wanted to stay home.

When you get a bad grade, you feel ashamed, and kinda sad.

When grades are good, you usually keep them good. If they're bad, then you usually keep them bad, and maybe worse.

These words suggest the great emotional involvement children, even very young children, can have in their grades. What is dangerous about this process is the assumption that children make about their own role in their education. Grades create the illusion that each individual alone is responsible for his or her accomplishments. If one works hard enough, listens in class, and does what he or she is told to do, then good grades will follow.

There is yet a subtler assumption that is evident here: *Everyone has the same capabilities. Children are born with the same skills and intelligence, so that when learning is not effective or integrated, it is the child's own fault. Teachers, school, family, and environment are only catalysts.* Everyone knows this is far from the truth. Children are different, often very different. What is helpful for one may not be helpful for another. Consequently, I am proposing that the responsibility for a child's accomplishments be shared among teachers, school, family, environment, and other influences related to education.

Sharing the Educational Burden

Society needs to take the burden of total responsibility for learning from the child. We need to share that burden. In order to demonstrate that belief, we should evaluate all the participants in the educational process *from the child's perspective.* It is not enough that cities and townships evaluate local schools or that principals assess their teaching staffs. The child has no part in that process; quite likely, she or he is not even aware that it is occurring. *What is important is that the child sometimes be given the role of evaluator.* Then, he or she may come to understand how a multiplicity of forces impinges on educational outcomes. Schools build their reputations by the quality of students they produce; they should also share the guilt when someone fails.

The student's evaluation of the teacher or the school in no way relieves the student of his or her own responsibility. This proposal is not intended to create scapegoats. It only suggests that children should not be given *total* educational responsibility, a situation that often results when students believe they are the only ones being evaluated. When the child has the opportunity to evaluate others, responsibility seems to be shared, although the student still maintains the major accountability for learning.

When the child becomes the evaluator, certain other advantages may result. For example, the child may learn to become a better observer. In questioning his or her teacher's behavior, he or she must become aware of what is useful and what is not. In questioning a fellow student, the child must know what is acceptable and what is not. He or she must think about what is happening and not accept it blindly. Thus, being the evaluator allows the child to develop a totally different perspective. The new role may allow children to learn more, and if nothing else, it may create in them more sympathy for the difficult role of any evaluator.

Evaluation by the Child

There are innumerable ways in which any child, even one of kindergarten age, can become an evaluator. It is possible for a child to evaluate himself or herself, one's peers, the teacher, the school, the community, and/or the family. For example, even very young children could talk about how they see themselves and what they think they are learning. For such children, who have not yet learned to write, a tape recorder or the teacher could receive and play back their ideas. Likewise, without writing, a young child could respond to a simple vocal questionnaire by placing checks next to pictures in a magazine or a workbook.

Another alternative is for the young child to draw pictures that represent one's family situation or one's fantasy of an ideal school. Games could even be utilized for evaluation purposes. Children could act like someone they admire at school. Maybe even for an entire day this role play could continue, allowing the children to feel what it is like to *be* someone else and to learn that they are capable of the same behavior as someone they admire. They could talk later about how easy or difficult it was, and how they felt about it generally. The child would also learn from such a situation, since he or she will confront his or her own criteria for respect.

Another game might be for young children to act out some symbols with their bodies (for example, the letters of the alphabet, or numbers), to learn if others can guess their identity. The evaluation following the game could be informal: Does being understood by others prove the success of one's efforts?

Interviewing is another technique that children of any age group could use to learn more from and about each other. In a small encounter where each child could feel at ease, it is possible that important information might be shared, not only among children, but also with the teacher.

Once the child can master writing, many other possibilities emerge. The child can fill out questionnaires evaluating the teacher, the school, and other components of the educational milieu. Interviews requiring note-taking can be conducted in school or outside of it. Students can read one another's papers, offer help, and receive suggestions. It is important to remember that nonverbal types of evaluation may also be useful with older children. Some older children may be able to express themselves more openly and capably in a drawing or a dramatization.

Choosing New Methods

As one can see, combinations for evaluation abound. One can alter the type of evaluation to match the person to be evaluated. Thus, many kinds of creative evaluations are possible.

Recipient of Evaluation	Type of Evaluation
Self	Structured-Unstructured
Peers	Verbal-Nonverbal
Teacher	Written-Spoken-Acted
School	Done Alone-Done with Others
Community	For Facts-For Feelings
Family	Etc.

Any combination of the above could offer some new ideas. For example, students could evaluate themselves by answering a structured questionnaire, drawing a picture, talking about themselves, asking others questions about themselves, and responding to the way others react to questions.

There has purposely been no attempt made to provide detailed instructions as to how any one of these evaluations might be specifically carried out. It is preferable that individual teachers formulate their own ideas to complement the unique needs of their classrooms. The suggestions given here are intended to inspire, not inhibit, imaginative possibilities. Both teachers and students often fail to realize the full extent of their creative capacities until challenged. Once we reject the constraining idea that only students are evaluated and that only teachers do the evaluating, we will realize the magnitude of creative combinations that can ensue.

Part II

The Arguments:
Researching the Myths,
Comparing the Alternatives

THERE ARE MANY myths surrounding grades. And myths die only slowly. In this section, the research about grades is discussed. Where did grades originate? How are they used? What are the good and bad effects of grades? In addition, this section provides a charted overview of the pro and con arguments about grades and the alternatives to grading systems.

What Research Says About Grading*

Francis B. Evans

THIS REVIEW OF the research on grading is selective rather than inclusive, and is intended to highlight points or directions the author deems important. Empirical research has been included wherever possible, and few philosophical or polemical sources have been cited.

For the purposes of this review, marks and grades are defined as single, summary symbols indicating achievement in some substantial segment of a student's educational enterprise (such as a course or a subject), given by the instructor for the purposes of record and report. The most common symbols employed at both the elementary and secondary levels are letter grades (A, B, C, D, and F).

Use of Grades Is Extensive

Estimates of the extent of letter grading in the public schools vary, but there is no question that grades are used in the majority of American schools. According to a National Education Association (NEA) survey, reported in a 1974 research summary,[1] letter grades were being used in 82 percent of the junior high schools and 84 percent of the senior high

* An earlier version of this article was prepared for an ad hoc committee examining marking and grading practices at the University of Wisconsin at Green Bay in 1972, while the author was chairperson of the committee. In organizing this overview, the author has relied heavily on an annotated bibliography included in: Howard Kirschenbaum, Sidney B. Simon, and Rodney W. Napier. *Wad-Ja-Get? The Grading Game in American Education.* New York: Hart Publishing Company, Inc., 1971.

[1] National Education Association. *What Research Says to the Teacher: Evaluation and Reporting of Student Achievement.* Washington, D.C.: the Association, 1974. Available from Educational Resources Information Center, U.S. Office of Education: ED 099 405.

schools sampled in 1971. Somewhat lower estimates were obtained for the number of schools using letter grades only.

In 1973, a five percent sample of school administrators—selected proportionally from both elementary and secondary school levels—was surveyed nationwide on the subject of grading. Fifty-nine percent of the respondents indicated that their districts *did not* use an evaluation system for students other than traditional report cards with letter grades or point averages.[2] Forty-one percent of the administrators indicated that their districts did employ other reporting systems; one-half of these districts used written evaluations by teachers and one-fourth used pass/fail evaluations.

A 1972 longitudinal study of grading practices at the high school level revealed that letter grades *only* were then being used by the majority (68 percent) of schools, and that reporting methods had remained nearly the same for at least a decade.[3]

In 1971, Oliver [4] reported that the vast majority of colleges were using letter grades, but noted that the majority were also using some form of non-traditional marking in their record keeping systems.

Dissatisfaction with Letter Grades

Neither teachers nor administrators are entirely satisfied with letter grades. The results of a teacher opinion poll, reported by NEA in 1971,[5] showed that the majority (52 percent) of both elementary and secondary teachers questioned were of the opinion that parent-teacher conferences are the best method of reporting pupil progress at the elementary level; only 16 percent believed letter grades to be the best reporting method for that level. For secondary level students, the opinions were more divided. The largest proportion (35 percent) of elementary and secondary teachers polled thought that letter grades are the best reporting method, but both teacher-parent conferences and pass/fail marks were

[2] Nation's Schools. "Schoolmen Don't Like'em But ABC Grades Linger On: School Administrators Opinion Poll." *Nation's Schools* 91: 52; March 1973.

[3] B. M. Pinchak and H. M. Breland. "Grading Practices in American High Schools: National Longitudinal Study of the High School Class of 1972." *Education Digest* 39: 21-23; March 1974.

[4] F. E. Oliver. *The AACRAO Survey of Grading Policies in Member Institutions.* Washington, D.C.: American Association of Collegiate Registrars and Admissions Officers, 1971. Cited in: David Otto. *Pass-Fail Grading Systems: A Literature Review.* Edmonton, Alberta, Canada: University of Alberta, Office of Institutional Research and Planning, September 1973. p. 31.

[5] National Education Association. "Reporting Pupil Progress to Parents." *National Education Association Research Bulletin* 49: 81-82; October 1971.

also favored, respectively, by 17 and 16 percent of those polled. The survey of elementary and secondary level school administrators mentioned earlier reported that 57 percent of the administrators responding were not satisfied with the grading system used in their districts.

There is evidence suggesting that students are socialized to accept grades at the elementary level, but that by the time they reach the high school level, they would prefer a marking system that would enable them to see themselves as distinct individuals. Chansky and Shaw [6] studied the preferences of equal-sized samples of students from the seventh, ninth, and twelfth grades of a Pennsylvania school system and found that the designations Honor/Good/Fair/Poor were rated highest when student responses were averaged across grade levels. Next in preference were contract grading and the designations Good/Satisfactory/Unsatisfactory. The researchers, finding that students at the higher grade levels preferred letter grades less than those at the lower levels, interpreted their data as suggesting that younger students accept, and approve of the available system, but older students prefer systems that enable them to see themselves as individuals.

Historical Perspective

A survey by Kirschenbaum, Simon, and Napier [7] of the history of grading and marking indicated that marking is a very recent educational phenomenon that developed in the last quarter of the nineteenth century.

Since the inception of grading, teachers have alternated between using scales with many gradations (such as 10-point and 100-point scales) and using two or three broad, evaluative categories (such as Outstanding, Average, and Needs Improvement). Shifts to different marking systems were reflections of changes in the prevailing educational philosophy over time.

Grading has long been the center of a storm of controversy, magnified by the early landmark research of Starch and Elliott,[8] which demonstrated the unreliability of teacher marks.

[6] N. M. Chansky and M. Shaw. "Development of Grading Preferences in High School Students." *Education* 93: 336-38; April 1973.

[7] Howard Kirschenbaum, Sidney B. Simon, and Rodney W. Napier. *Wad-Ja-Get? The Grading Game in American Education.* New York: Hart Publishing Company, Inc., 1971.

[8] D. Starch and E. Elliott. "Reliability of the Grading of High School Work in English." *School Review* 20: 442-57; 1912; *idem,* "Reliability of Grading Work in Mathematics." *School Review* 21: 254-95; 1913, and "Reliability of Grading Work in History." *School Review* 21: 676-81; 1913.

The 1960's brought a renewed reaction to grading. The plea for more humanized educational approaches voiced in *Perceiving, Behaving, Becoming* [9] has been picked up and reiterated. Books on individualizing instruction, such as Bishop's *Individualizing Educational Systems*,[10] have questioned grading practices on the grounds that they stifle the development of a truly individualized learning approach. Recent papers, such as that given by Leuba,[11] also argue that letter grades and individualized instruction are incompatible.

Often grading has appeared on the list of school activities that critics view as dehumanizing to education, but seldom have critics included supportive research in their contention. The Association for Supervision and Curriculum Development's 1967 Yearbook, *Evaluation as Feedback and Guide*,[12] strongly criticizes grades, for example, but does not cite the research supporting these criticisms. It is hoped that the following review of the research related to marking and grading will help to strengthen the important conclusions presented in this ASCD publication.

Functions Ascribed to Grades

Over twenty years ago, Wrinkle [13] listed four functions of marks.

1. *Administrative Functions:* Marks indicate whether a student has passed or failed, whether he or she should be promoted or required to repeat the grade or course, and whether he or she should be graduated. They are used in transferring a student from one school to another and in judging candidates for admission to college. They may be used by employers in evaluating prospective employees.

[9] Arthur W. Combs, chairman, ASCD 1962 Yearbook Committee. *Perceiving, Behaving, Becoming: A New Focus for Education.* Washington, D.C.: Association for Supervision and Curriculum Development, 1962.

[10] L. K. Bishop. *Individualizing Educational Systems.* New York: Harper & Row, Publishers, 1971.

[11] R. J. Leuba. "Individualized Instruction and the Letter Grade System." Paper presented at the National Conference on Behavior Research and Technology in Higher Education, Atlanta, Georgia, November 14-16, 1974. Available from Educational Resources Information Center, U.S. Office of Education: ED 100 308.

[12] Fred T. Wilhelms, editor. *Evaluation as Feedback and Guide.* Washington, D.C.: Association for Supervision and Curriculum Development, 1967.

[13] W. L. Wrinkle. *Improving Marking and Reporting Practices in Elementary and Secondary Schools.* New York: Holt, Rinehart and Winston, Inc., 1947. Copyright 1947 by Holt, Rinehart and Winston, Inc., and reprinted with permission.

2. *Guidance Functions:* Marks are used in guidance and counseling in identifying areas of special ability and inability, in deciding on the advisability of enrolling the student in certain courses and keeping him or her out of others, and in determining the number of courses in which he or she may be enrolled.

3. *Information Functions:* Marks are the chief means employed by the school in giving information to students and their parents regarding the student's achievement, progress, and success or failure in his or her schoolwork.

4. *Motivation and Discipline Functions:* Marks are used to stimulate students to make greater effort in their learning activities. They are used for the same purpose in determining eligibility for honors of many different kinds, such as participation in group activities, eligibility to play on the team, and membership in selected groups.

The research findings about marking and grading will be examined in relation to these four functions Wrinkle ascribed to grades.

Administrative Functions

Predicting College Performance: Although it is contended that a student's past academic record is a good indicator of his or her probable future performance, it is not as good a predictor as many educators believe. Typical studies, such as those by Hills, Klock, and Bush [14] and by Klugh and Bierley,[15] indicate that at the secondary level, grades received one year typically correlate about 0.60 with the subsequent year's grades, and that high school rank in class correlates slightly over 0.60 with college grades. This means that slightly over one-third of the variation in a student's academic performance can be accounted for by prior marks. Moreover, a study at the University of Michigan found that, from a financial point of view, it is more practical for college admissions officers to study each applicant individually rather than to use gross screening procedures based on grade point average and high school rank.[16]

[14] J. Hills, J. Klock, and M. Bush. "The Use of Academic Prediction Equations with Subsequent Classes." *American Educational Research Journal* 2: 203-206; 1965.

[15] H. Klugh and R. Bierley. "The School and College Ability Test and High School Grades as Predictors of Achievement." *Educational and Psychological Measurement* 19: 625-26; 1959.

[16] S. Miller. *Measure, Number, and Weight: A Polemical Statement of the College Grading Problem.* Ann Arbor, Michigan: University of Michigan, Center of Research on Learning and Teaching, 1967. Cited in: Howard Kirschenbaum, Sidney B. Simon, and Rodney W. Napier. *Wad-Ja-Get? The Grading Game in American Education.* New York: Hart Publishing Company, Inc., 1971. p. 273.

Predicting Professional Performance: Grades in a particular occupational field show almost no relationship to subsequent occupational success. Barr,[17] summarizing 33 studies of teacher effectiveness, found that college grade point averages of teachers had a median correlation of 0.09 with later on-the-job ratings given by their supervisors.

In medicine, there is a similar lack of relationship between grades and subsequent professional success. Prince [18] found a slight relationship between medical school grades and early success in the profession, and no relationship in the long run between grades and a list of 24 performance characteristics of physicians.

Even in a highly specific skills-oriented field such as engineering, little relationship has been shown to exist between grades and eventual success, according to research by Martin and Pacheres.[19] Their study also found that there was no relationship between grades and on-the-job salaries of engineers.

Hoyt, after reviewing 46 studies that have investigated the relationship between college grades and various measures of later success, concluded:

Although this area of research is plagued by many theoretical, experimental, measurement, and statistical difficulties, present evidence strongly suggests that college grades bear little or no relationship to any measures of adult accomplishment.[20]

How Employers and Graduate Schools View Grades: Grades do not appear to serve well for administrative functions. They are only moderately good predictors of future success in school, and they apparently bear little or no relation to future success beyond school. However, grades may still be viewed as important by employers and graduate schools.

[17] A. S. Barr *et al. Wisconsin Studies of the Measurement and Prediction of Teacher Effectiveness.* Madison: Dembar Publications, 1961.

[18] P. B. Prince, C. W. Taylor, J. M. Richards, Jr., and T. L. Jacobsen. *Performance Measures of Physicians.* Final report submitted to the U.S. Office of Education, Washington, D.C., 1963. Cited in: *Degrading Education.* Washington, D.C.: National Student Association, Center for Educational Reform, 1969; and in: Howard Kirschenbaum, Sidney B. Simon, and Rodney W. Napier. *Wad-Ja-Get? The Grading Game in American Education.* New York: Hart Publishing Company, Inc., 1971. p. 282.

[19] R. A. Martin and J. Pacheres. "Good Scholars Not Always the Best." Cited in: *Business Week;* February 24, 1962. pp. 77-78; and in: Howard Kirschenbaum, Sidney B. Simon, and Rodney W. Napier. *Wad-Ja-Get? The Grading Game in American Education.* New York: Hart Publishing Company, Inc., 1971. p. 282.

[20] D. P. Hoyt. *The Relationship Between College Grades and Adult Achievement: A Review of the Literature.* ACT Research Report No. 7. Iowa City, Iowa: American College Testing Program, 1965.

Employers in business and government have said they consider grades to be second in importance only to previous work experience in evaluating prospective employees, according to a survey taken in the Chicago region.[21] That employers may look closely at grades was also demonstrated in a recent survey of school superintendents regarding their screening of job applicants.[22] The respondents indicated that an applicant's chance for employment *decreased* when non-traditional grades exceeded ten percent of his or her course work. (When non-traditional grades represented less than ten percent of the individual's academic work, chance for employment would not be significantly reduced.)

Non-traditional grades can also have a negative effect on graduate school opportunities. According to a study by Schoemer and others,[23] if more than ten percent of a student's college record is made up of non-traditional grades, chance for admission to graduate school and opportunities for financial aid may be sharply reduced.

Guidance Functions

Is an A Always an A? All of the research cited in the section on the administrative functions of grades could be cited here as well. However, there are other problems with using grades for guidance purposes in addition to that of their low predictive validity. These problems center around what an A or B means when given by different instructors, and around the unreliability of grading procedures themselves. Chansky,[24] analyzing the use of grade point average in research, has pointed out how grades can represent different things to different teachers. Chamberlin [25] has commented that the proportion of A's given has varied

21 R. L. Bailey. *AACRAO Subcommittee on Non-Traditional Grading Patterns.* Park Forest South, Illinois: Governors State University, Office of Admissions & Records, 1972. Mimeograph. Cited in: D. Otto. *Pass-Fail Grading Systems: A Literature Review.* Edmonton, Alberta, Canada: University of Alberta, Office of Institutional Research and Planning, September 1973. p. 7. Available from Educational Resources Information Center, U.S. Office of Education: ED 109 209.

22 J. E. Thomas *et al.* "Effects of Non-Traditional Grades on Hiring Practices of School Systems." *Journal of Educational Measurement* 11: 213-17; Fall 1974.

23 J. R. Schoemer *et al.* "Study of the Effect of Non-Traditional Grades on Admission to Graduate School and the Awarding of Financial Assistance." *College and University* 48: 147-53; Spring 1973.

24 N. M. Chansky. "A Note on the Grade Point Average in Research." *Educational and Psychological Measurement* 24 (1): 95-99; 1964.

25 C. Chamberlin, E. S. Chamberlin, N. E. Drought, and W. E. Scott. *Did They Succeed in College?* Adventure in American Education, Volume IV. New York: Harper & Row, Publishers, 1942.

not only from college to college, department to department, and instructor to instructor, but also when the same instructor has graded the same materials at different times.

Irregularities in the assignment of grades are highlighted by a Temple University ad hoc committee study [26] that found dramatic differences in grade distributions, not only among different colleges and departments within the university, but even among different professors teaching the same course. For example, in one course with a total enrollment of 514 students, an instructor of a section with 34 students gave no A's, while 67 percent of the students received D's or F's. Another instructor, teaching 30 students, gave no F's, while 63 percent of the students received A's or B's. In this case, a student's choice of instructor (actually, there really was no choice since students were assigned randomly within their time demands) may prove to have long-range effects on his or her future.

A similar discrepancy in grade distributions was found at San Diego State College by Kirby.[27] Analyzing the grades awarded by 206 lower division instructors, he found that the median grades they awarded ranged from below C (1.82) to nearly A (3.88). A similarly wide range was reported for upper division instructors as well.

However, Otto [28] conducted an analysis similar to Chamberlin's 1942 study and found relatively little year-to-year variation or department-to-department variation in three colleges. Otto commented further that the grade distributions were remarkably stable from year to year. Also, research has shown that overall grade point average is not markedly affected by the differing standards employed in various courses.[29]

Teacher Judgments Vary: Course grades are usually a combination of test results (of varying reliability and validity) and teacher judgments as to student effort, punctuality, behavior, neatness of work, and how

[26] Temple University. *Report of the College of Education Ad Hoc Committee on Grading Systems.* "In-house" report. Philadelphia, Pennsylvania: Temple University, 1968. Cited in: Howard Kirschenbaum, Sidney B. Simon, and Rodney W. Napier. *Wad-Ja-Get? The Grading Game in American Education.* New York: Hart Publishing Company, Inc., 1971. pp. 259-61.

[27] B. C. Kirby. "Three Error Sources in College Grades." *Journal of Experimental Education* 31: 213-18; 1962.

[28] David Otto. *Pass-Fail Grading Systems: A Literature Review.* Edmonton, Alberta, Canada: University of Alberta, Office of Institutional Research and Planning, September 1973. Available from Educational Resources Information Center, U.S. Office of Education: ED 109 209.

[29] A. F. Etaugh, C. F. Etaugh, and D. E. Hurd. "Reliability of College Grades and Grade Point Averages: Some Implications for Predicting Academic Performance." *Educational and Psychological Measurement* 32: 1045-1050; 1972.

well the student is "working up to capacity." [30] Usually, these non-test aspects are given much more weight in elementary school than in high school or college. However, because course grades do reflect a degree of teacher judgment, research on the unreliability of judgments made by teachers grading individual papers is relevant.

Until the landmark research of Starch and Elliott mentioned earlier, teacher judgment of student work was practically unquestioned. However, in three simply designed studies, these researchers demonstrated that teachers of high school English, geometry, and history—even when grading the same paper—arrived at markedly different evaluations. For each of these subjects, approximately 100 teachers were asked to mark a paper on a scale of 100 points, with 75 points being a passing mark. In English, a range of 39 points was found. Critics argued that since English is a subjective area of study, the findings were not surprising, but they were astonished when similar variability—a range of about 45 points—was found in geometry. These studies were landmarks in casting doubt on the reliability of testing and grading procedures, as they demonstrated that the variability in marks was not a function of the subject area, but appeared to be a function of the grader.

A later study by Bells [31] demonstrated that teachers, when requested to regrade a series of geography and history examinations, did so with low reliability. Tieg [32] reported that a single teacher, given the same test papers to rescore after a two-month interval, assigned marks that differed 14 points on the average (on a 100-point scale) from the marks first assigned. Bracht [33] found that the first and second scores given to a single, brief essay question correlated 0.50 when reread by the same instructor, and 0.47 when read by a different instructor.

Thus, other than being only moderately good predictors of future achievement, grades do not serve guidance functions well. Not only do

[30] J. C. Stanley and K. D. Hopkins. *Educational and Psychological Measurement and Evaluation.* Englewood Cliffs, New Jersey: Prentice-Hall, Inc., 1972. Chapter 13.

[31] W. C. Bells. "Reliability of Repeated Grading of Essay Type Examinations." *Journal of Educational Psychology* 21: 48-52; 1930.

[32] E. W. Tieg. *Educational Diagnosis.* Bulletin No. 18. Monterey, California: California Testing Bureau, 1952. Cited in: Howard Kirschenbaum, Sidney B. Simon, and Rodney W. Napier. *Wad-Ja-Get? The Grading Game in American Education.* New York: Hart Publishing Company, Inc., 1971. pp. 261-62.

[33] G. H. Bracht. "The Comparative Values of Objective and Essay Testing in Undergraduate Education: Implications for Valid Assessment of Instruction." Unpublished master's thesis. Denver: University of Colorado, 1967. Cited in: J. C. Stanley and K. D. Hopkins. *Educational and Psychological Measurement and Evaluation.* Englewood Cliffs, New Jersey: Prentice-Hall, Inc., 1972. p. 203.

they have low predictive validity for vocational success, but they are also unreliable and often loaded with subjectivity.

Information Functions

Arbitrary Criteria Employed: In light of the above research, the information content of grades and marks must be considered low. The NEA survey of teachers referred to earlier indicated that less than half of those questioned believed grades to be the best method of reporting student achievement. The questionable information content of a "passing" or "non-passing" mark is also supported by the findings of Adams,[34] who surveyed teachers to determine what level of performance or behavior they felt warranted a failing grade. Responses indicated that teachers evaluated students in varied and sometimes non-measurable ways. Some said, for example, that they would fail a student who "shows no interest," "is not paying attention," "has too many absences," or "is not meeting certain specific academic standards." Adams found that specific criteria were rare, and he revealed how arbitrary the factors underlying a failing grade can be. The tragedy underscored by this study is that even though the criteria used were arbitrary and may have changed with time, the "failure" will remain permanently on the student's record.

It is well known that passing or even high grades do not indicate the specific skills and knowledge acquired by the student receiving the grades. A grade of A or B awarded by an instructor at a given institution is not necessarily comparable to the same grade awarded by instructors in other departments and is certainly not comparable to grades awarded by other institutions.

Researchers Goldman and Hewitt,[35] analyzing data from four different universities in California, found that academic fields accepting students with lower abilities tend to award grades less stringently than fields enrolling students with higher abilities.

Grades Awarded Over Time: Grades probably should be interpreted in light of the years in which they were awarded. For example, during the 1950's and 1960's, aptitude test scores increased, but grade distributions remained unchanged. One of the early studies demonstrating that average grades remained unchanged despite rising SAT scores was performed by Aiken.[36] One of the last major studies of this

[34] W. L. Adams. "Why Teachers Say They Fail Students." *Educational Administration and Supervision* 18: 594-600; 1932.

[35] R. D. Goldman and B. N. Hewitt. "Adaptation-Level as an Explanation for Differential Standards in College Grading." *Journal of Educational Measurement* 12: 149-61; Fall 1975.

[36] L. R. Aiken. "The Grading Behavior of a College Faculty." *Educational and Psychological Measurement* 23: 319-22; 1963.

era was conducted by Baird and Feister, who analyzed data collected from a large sample of colleges during 1964-68. They concluded:

This study confirms the earlier research . . . which indicated that faculty members, at least collectively, prefer or are committed to a certain distribution of grades. Thus, faculties show an "adaptation level" by awarding, on the average, about the same average and distribution of grades, whether their current students were brighter or duller than last year's.[37]

However, toward the end of the 1960's, the situation changed. Aptitude test scores started dropping and the average grades awarded to students started increasing. As of 1975, it was reported that one-half to two-thirds of the marks given in U.S. colleges and universities were A's and B's, even though aptitude scores had dropped slowly but steadily during the previous ten years.[38] A similar, though not quite so strong, grade inflation is now occurring in high schools.[39]

Thus, A's or B's awarded in college in the early 1960's probably do not represent the same student achievement level as the same grades awarded in the late 1960's (because they were earned when a different level of competition prevailed), and the same grades awarded now certainly are not comparable to earlier grades.

Motivation and Discipline Functions

Students Respond to Grades Differently: Contrary to popular opinion, there is little evidence that grades supply strong positive motivation for most students. Usually the only students who find grades motivating are the better students. For example, Phillips [40] reported that anxiety increased the grades of students who were already receiving good

---

[37] Leonard L. Baird and William J. Feister. "Grading Standards: The Relation of Changes in Average Student Ability to the Average Grades Awarded." *American Educational Research Journal,* Volume 9; Summer 1972, p. 440. Copyright 1972, American Educational Research Association, Washington, D.C.

[38] J. F. Davidson. "Academic Interest Rates and Grade Inflation." *Educational Record* 56: 122-25; Spring 1975. See also: R. F. Grose and R. C. Butler. "Grading Game." *College and University* 50: 723-39; Summer 1975.

[39] R. L. Ferguson and E. J. Maxey. "Trends in the Academic Performance of High School and College Students." Paper presented at the 50th Annual Convention of the American College Personnel Association, Atlanta, Georgia, March 5-8, 1975. Available from Educational Resources Information Center, U.S. Office of Education: ED 109 523.

[40] B. Phillips. "Sex, Social Class, and Anxiety as Sources of Variation in School Anxiety." *Journal of Educational Psychology* 53: 316-22; 1962; *idem,* "The Classroom: A Place To Learn." In: D. H. Clark and G. S. Lesser, editors. *Emotional Disturbance and School Learning.* Chicago: Science Research Associates, 1965. pp. 263-64.

grades, but lowered the grades of students whose previous performance was average. Brim [41] reported that grades are one of the major influences in shaping a student's estimate of his or her own ability, and McDavid [42] suggested that academic success may result in a more positive self-image which, in turn, may lead to a student's increased success in school.

Chansky,[43] in examining the issues causing a reconsideration of grading practices, pointed out that although educators often view grades as motivating factors, research suggests that down-graded students often continue to fail. He also noted that students have responded to test anxiety in different ways. For some, it has increased performance, but for others, it may lead to withdrawal and a sense of defeat. Chansky also pointed out that although, in theory, students who receive poor grades on an examination should review materials and retake the exam to demonstrate their increased proficiency, this seldom happens since the class moves on whether or not the student has achieved the needed level of competence.

According to more recent research, low grades can have differential effects. Thayer [44] reported that college students receiving D's and F's during a course dropped out more frequently than other students, but he noted that the low-graded students who continued the course performed better on a subsequent exam. Thayer also found that students receiving A's on the first exam scored significantly higher on the second. This finding supports McDavid's contention mentioned earlier.

Students Can Progress Without Grades: It has often been argued that the motivational value of grades is so important that, despite the other problems associated with them, their use must be continued.

Supporters of marks and grades argue that if grades were eliminated, students would not work. Research does not support this contention and, in fact, a study by Chamberlin and others [45] demonstrated that the reverse could be true.

Chamberlin's study is so important that it deserves a detailed treatment. The aim of the experiment was to determine just how important

[41] O. G. Brim, D. A. Goslin, D. C. Glass, and I. Goldberg. *The Use of Standardized Ability Tests in American Secondary Schools.* New York: Russell Sage Foundation, 1964.

[42] John McDavid. "Some Relationships Between Social Reinforcement and Scholastic Achievement." *Journal of Consulting Psychology* 23: 151-54; 1959.

[43] N. M. Chansky. "The X-Ray of the School Mark." *Educational Forum;* March 1962. pp. 347-52.

[44] R. E. Thayer. "Do Low Grades Cause College Students To Give Up?" *Journal of Experimental Education* 41: 71-73; Spring 1973.

[45] See footnote reference 25 cited earlier.

a rigid college-oriented high school curriculum, including grades, was to a student's later success in college. During an eight-year period beginning in 1932, nearly 1,500 students from 30 "test" high schools were matched with an equal sample of other students on a number of educationally important variables. These variables included age, sex, religion, socioeconomic background, previous grade average, and others.

One group of schools—the experimental group—was allowed almost a free hand in determining how it would develop its college preparatory programs. Many eliminated grading. Schools in the second group—the control group—offered typical college preparatory programs that included grading.

Three hundred cooperating colleges agreed to accept students from the experimental schools on the basis of recommendations from the principals. On the measures employed during college, students from this group performed as well as or better than those in the control group. They earned slightly better grades in all subject fields except foreign language and were judged to be more intellectually curious, resourceful, and more objective in their thinking.

Chamberlin's study, which has never been replicated, demonstrated that grading was not essential to motivate students. On the contrary, the results suggest that grading could be a hindrance to the development of intellectual and personal skills.

More recently, Butterworth and Michael [46] pointed out that an individualized narrative evaluation of the work of sixth-grade students resulted in the students' attaining higher reading achievement and a greater sense of self-responsibility. In this study, two samples (300 students in each group), comparable in socioeconomic and ethnic composition, received different forms of evaluation. The members of the control group received typical letter grades (A-F) on their work, while the experimental students had their work judged and reported according to an individualized narrative form without grades or symbols. (The research does not mention the comparability of the instruction the two groups received, so it is possible that the results were a function of instructional as well as reporting differences. However, the results at least are encouraging.)

Negative Motivational Effects: Marking and grading have been found to have several undesirable motivational effects. For example,

[46] T. W. Butterworth and W. B. Michael. "Relationship of Reading Achievement, School Attitude, and Self-Responsible Behaviors of Sixth-Grade Pupils to Comparative and Individualized Reporting Systems: Implications for Improvement of Validity of the Evaluation of Pupil Progress." *Educational and Psychological Measurement* 35: 987-91; Winter 1975.

they produce conformity, reduce teacher-student interaction, and encourage students to cheat to assure passing grades.

Bostrom [47] found that grades can be used to shape student opinions in the forms of their expressed beliefs. Lippitt [48] reported that elementary students, although they will confide privately that they have a strong desire to be more active and cooperative with the teacher, will not be so, because they perceive that most of their peers are against such cooperation; they also recognize that group consensus does not support students who are too eager about studying.

Bowers,[49] reporting on a nationwide survey of college students, found that at least 50 percent admitted they had cheated during college by plagiarizing, using crib notes, copying on an examination, and by using other means. Bowers commented that all of these illegitimate actions were a consequence of the system of examinations and grade points, and that students engage in cheating because they believe they may be rewarded by a higher grade.

A similar situation was reported by Fala, who noted that at least half of the 5,000 college students interviewed during a study by the Columbia University Bureau of Applied Social Research admitted to cheating. He indicated that the incidence of cheating was highest among weak students, men, career-oriented majors, and students who were in school for such non-academic interests as sports and music. Fala concluded:

> We are faced with the inescapable fact that any time we receive a set of term papers, a substantial proportion of them will be the product of one of the numerous intra- or inter-campus term paper rings which, to those interested in criminal syndicalism and white collar crime, are among the more fascinating and exotic of the innovative adoptions of students.[50]

[47] R. N. Bostrom, J. W. Vlandis, and M. E. Rosenbaum. "Grades as Reinforcing Contingencies and Attitude Change." *Journal of Educational Psychology* 52: 112-15; 1961.

[48] Ronald Lippitt. "Unplanned Maintenance and Planned Change in the Group Work Process." In: *Social Work Practice*. New York: Columbia University Press, 1962.

[49] William Bowers. *Student Dishonesty and Its Control in College*. New York: New York Bureau of Applied Behavioral Science, 1964. Cited in: Howard Becker *et al. Making the Grade: The Academic Side of College Life.* New York: John Wiley & Sons, Inc., 1968. pp. 101-102.

[50] M. A. Fala. *Dunce Caps, Hickory Sticks, and Public Evaluations: The Structure of Academic Authoritarianism.* Madison: University of Wisconsin, Teaching Assistant Association, 1968. Cited in: Howard Kirschenbaum, Sidney B. Simon, and Rodney W. Napier. *Wad-Ja-Get? The Grading Game in American Education.* New York: Hart Publishing Company, Inc., 1971. p. 268.

The proportion of students who cheat may be well over 50 percent. Knowlton and Hamerlynck [51] surveyed students from two universities: one a small, rural liberal arts college and the other a large metropolitan university. Eighty-one percent of the students surveyed at one college admitted to cheating, with 46 percent of them admitting they had cheated that very semester. At the other college, 47 percent indicated they profited from cheating and only 35 percent indicated that they did not cheat. In an earlier study by Canning,[52] 81 percent of the students at a large university indicated they cheated. Later, after an honors system had been well established, the degree of cheating dropped to 30 percent.

This dismal set of research findings offers fairly conclusive evidence that grading and marking, as currently practiced, fulfill few if any of the positive motivational and disciplinary functions ascribed to them.

Considering Some Alternatives

Research on attempts to mitigate the effects of marking and grading is sparse, and the findings do not suggest a clear direction in which to proceed. Some alternatives that have been employed include blanket grading, pass/fail marking, mastery learning, and contract grading.

Blanket Grading and Pass/Fail Marking

The following research findings suggest that both blanket grading and pass/fail options have decided weaknesses when incorporated into a system in which most of the courses are graded.

Weakness of Blanket Grading: Clark [53] compared graduate students enrolled in an advanced educational psychology course, in which a grade of B was guaranteed, with graduate students taking a similar course on a regularly graded basis. Although he found that the students in the course that was graded competitively wrote much better research papers, and reported that they spent a greater number of hours studying, he discerned no difference between the performance of each group on a final examination. The students in the course with a guaranteed grade claimed that pressure for grades in other courses caused them to let the

[51] J. Q. Knowlton and L. A. Hamerlynck. "Perception of Deviant Behavior: A Study of Cheating." *Journal of Educational Psychology* 58: 379-85; December 1967.

[52] R. R. Canning. "Does an Honor System Reduce Classroom Cheating?" *Journal of Experimental Education* 23: 291-96; June 1956.

[53] D. C. Clark. "Competition for Grades and Graduate-Student Performance." *Journal of Educational Research* 62: 351-54; April 1969.

psychology course slide, and that they found it difficult to muster motivation.

Marshall and Christensen [54] reported on a small study of high school students that revealed no significant differences between control and experimental groups in either achievement or achievement motivation, when one of the groups received regular grades on class work, and the other received "lenient marks," which had been systematically raised one level. Thus, at least over one semester, strict grading did not appear to be necessary to maintain achievement or motivation.

Effects of Pass/Fail in Colleges: Pass/fail marking has been used at the college level in the hope that it would encourage students to explore academic areas unfamiliar to them and would reduce their anxiety about grades. A study by Bain and others [55] indicated pass/fail marking reduced anxiety, but that few students elected pass/fail for exploration of an unfamiliar academic area. In fact, 87 percent of the students Bain polled reported that they elected pass/fail marking either to provide more study time for other courses or to protect their grade point averages when taking a difficult course. Furthermore, about one-third of the students electing pass/fail reported a lowering of motivation, while only 12 percent experienced an increase in motivation. Similarly, one-fourth of the students felt that they learned less in pass/fail courses, and only 13 percent reported that they learned more. Thus, while pass/fail marking reduced anxiety about grades in the students Bain questioned, it often was used to protect grade point averages, and it seldom was used by the students to explore new areas. Furthermore, while the majority of the students electing pass/fail marking reported that their levels of motivation and the amount they learned were unchanged, a substantial minority reported reductions in these areas.

Gold and others [56] analyzed complete pass/fail marking (that is, all courses taken by the student that semester were pass/fail), partial pass/fail marking, and traditional grading. It was found: (a) that students preferred the idea of partial pass/fail marking to the other two methods, and (b) that pass/fail grading led to a decline in academic performance. Even after returning to conventional grading, the students who had taken all courses pass/fail for one year received significantly

[54] J. C. Marshall and D. L. Christensen. "Leniency in Marking: Its Effects on Student Motivation and Achievement." *Education* 93: 362-65; February 1973.

[55] P. T. Bain, L. W. Hales, and L. P. Rand. "Does Pass-Fail Encourage Exploration?" *College and University* 47: 17-18; Fall 1971.

[56] R. M. Gold, A. Reilly, R. Silberman, and R. Lehr. "Academic Achievement Declined Under Pass/Fail Grading." *Journal of Experimental Education* 39: 17-21; Spring 1971.

lower grades than students in the control group.

Reviews by Pedrini and Pedrini [57] and by Otto [58] have shown that pass/fail marking has gained wide acceptance among college students, and that the general practice in many colleges and universities is to limit the number of pass/fail courses a student may take. The reviews suggest that students often use the pass/fail system to redistribute time and effort in such a way as to concentrate on the courses elected under the conventional grading system. Some students use pass/fail marking as a means of carrying an extra course or two, but more often, they use it to redistribute academic effort, and in a good proportion of the cases, student achievement in the pass/fail courses is adversely affected.

Effects of Pass/Fail in High Schools: At the high school level, less research has been reported and it appears that pass/fail marking has not been tried as often as at the college level.

Bishop [59] described an effort to implement pass/fail marking in a California high school during the 1967-68 school year. Only electives (that is, courses not required for graduation or college entrance) were offered on an optional pass/fail basis. Both the conventional letter grade system and the pass/fail system operated concurrently, and neither teachers nor students were required to choose one or the other. Furthermore, the number of courses a student could take during a semester on pass/fail was limited: It was possible to take a total of nine courses, and at least five of them had to be on a letter grade basis.

According to Bishop, a year-end survey indicated that about 60 percent of the students felt they had worked as hard or harder on their pass/fail courses than on other courses, while nearly 40 percent felt they had exerted somewhat less effort on pass/fail courses. Only five percent of the students felt they had received less value from the pass/fail courses than from other courses, whereas about 60 percent felt they had received the same value, and nearly 30 percent felt they had received more. Both teacher and student reactions to the pass/fail system were positive. However, the effects of pressure on students to achieve good grades in traditional courses were present: 44 percent of the students said that they had chosen pass/fail marking to relieve the pressure of letter grades. These findings are remarkably similar to the college-level findings reported by Bain, which were presented earlier.

[57] B. C. Pedrini and D. T. Pedrini. *Pass-Fail Grading: Summary and Tentative Conclusions.* Omaha, Nebraska: University of Nebraska at Omaha, 1972. Available from Educational Resources Information Center, U.S. Office of Education: ED 080 073.

[58] See footnote reference 28 cited earlier.

[59] Bishop, *op. cit.*, pp. 192-99.

However, somewhat conflicting results appear in an article by Weber [60] referring to a 1972 study at the high school level involving a comparison between students who elected courses on a pass/fail basis and students who received letter grades. Both groups were assigned letter grades by teachers, who did not know which of their students were taking a course on a pass/fail basis. Counselors later converted these grades to pass/fail designations for the experimental students. It was found that the group electing pass/fail was assigned lower letter grades by teachers than the control group. Thus, it appears as if achievement may be reduced in pass/fail courses at the high school level.

It should be emphasized that most of the studies mentioned here examined the effects of blanket grading and pass/fail marking within systems where most courses were graded competitively. It appears that introducing a change into part of the system, while leaving the rest unchanged, may produce undesirable results because of the pressure the student feels to achieve good grades in other courses.

Mastery Learning

One promising instructional approach, which could have considerable impact on current marking practices, has been evolved from a model of mastery learning proposed by Carroll.[61] This mastery-learning approach is based on the assumption that what is commonly called "aptitude" determines the student's rate of learning, but not necessarily the learning ceiling, and that most, if not all, students can achieve mastery of a given subject if the instructional approaches are matched to individual needs and if each student is permitted to progress at his or her own pace. This assumption has been supported at least partially by research conducted by Atkinson [62] and by Glaser,[63] which demonstrated

[60] C. A. Weber. "Pass-Fail: Does It Work?" *Bulletin of the National Association of Secondary School Principals* 58: 104-106; April 1974.

[61] J. A. Carroll. "A Model of School Learning." *Teachers College Record* 64: 723-33; 1963.

[62] R. C. Atkinson. *Computerized Instruction and the Learning Process.* Technical Report No. 122. Stanford, California: Institute for Mathematical Studies in the Social Sciences, 1967. Cited in: B. S. Bloom, J. T. Hastings, and G. F. Madaus. *Handbook on Formative and Summative Evaluation of Student Learning.* New York: McGraw-Hill Book Company, 1971. p. 46.

[63] R. Glaser. "Adapting the Elementary School Curriculum to Individual Performance." In: *Proceedings of the 1967 Invitational Conference on Testing Problems.* Princeton, New Jersey: Educational Testing Service, 1968. pp. 3-36. Cited in: B. S. Bloom *et al. Handbook on Formative and Summative Evaluation of Student Learning.* New York: McGraw-Hill Book Company, 1971. p. 46.

that when students were allowed to learn at their own rates, most of them eventually attained mastery of each learning task, although some achieved mastery much sooner than others.

Airasian,[64] one instructor who attempted to implement mastery-learning approaches at the college level, reported gratifying results. Before Airasian introduced mastery strategies to a course on test theory, approximately 20 percent of the students were receiving the grade of A on the final examination. After implementation, student performance on the final exams increased dramatically. At the end of the first year of implementation, 80 percent of the students attained A level scores on a parallel form of the final exam. Two years after the strategy had been implemented, 90 percent of the students taking the course attained an A achievement level and were awarded A's on the final exam. The implementation of mastery-learning strategies can result in a very large proportion of students receiving A's, as this case shows. Since a considerable number of teachers become very uncomfortable when large numbers of students receive A's, the use of mastery-learning strategies could have dramatic effects on current marking practices.

Contract Grading

Contract grading is a method whereby the student and teacher agree upon what the student must do in order to receive a given grade. The method can be applied to a whole class, or to any number of students on an individual basis. Ideally, the contract should also include a statement of how the quality of the student's work will be judged and what levels of proficiency are necessary to earn a given grade. If these features are included, then contract grading is related to mastery learning.

One small study at the college level performed by Newcomb and Warmbrod [65] compared a regularly graded class with a class in which individuals had contracted for grades. During the fall quarter, both classes had similar grade distributions, but during the winter quarter, the "contract-graded" class received higher grades. In both quarters, the

[64] P. W. Airasian. "An Application of a Modified Version of John Carroll's Model of School Learning." Unpublished master's thesis. Chicago: University of Chicago, 1967. Cited in: B. S. Bloom, J. T. Hastings, and G. F. Madaus. *Handbook on Formative and Summative Evaluation of Student Learning*. New York: McGraw-Hill Book Company, 1971. p. 55.

[65] L. H. Newcomb and J. R. Warmbrod. *The Effect of Contract Grading on Student Performance*. Part of a series, *Summary of Research*. Columbus, Ohio: Ohio State University, Department of Agricultural Education, 1974. Available from Educational Resources Information Center, U.S. Office of Education: ED 093 967.

contract-graded and regularly graded students displayed nearly the same attitudes toward the course, the instructor, the exams used, and the teaching methods employed. The amount of reading students from both groups did for the course was also essentially the same. However, the investigators did question whether the regularly graded class really had been taught like a typical course, since students could complete extra projects—with the instructor's permission—to raise their grades.

Two studies at the secondary level reported that students receiving grades on a contract basis demonstrated similar achievement levels and similar attitudes toward the class. Ball [66] found this to be true for two ninth-grade general math classes, which were compared to two control classes. Two teachers were involved, each teaching one experimental and one control class. Yarber [67] reported similar findings for a ninth-grade health course, when comparing the attitudes and performance levels exhibited by two regularly graded classes and two contract-graded classes during a study unit on VD that lasted for nine class sessions. Both of these studies suggest that contract grading is at least as good as, if not better than, regular grading.

Conclusions

This survey of the research about the effects of marking and grading suggests that the traditional letter-grade system has more drawbacks and disadvantages than positive features. Although many of the studies examined in this article were conducted more than twenty years ago, there is little reason to believe that replication of them would result in different conclusions, since teacher marking and grading practices have not changed significantly.

It is clear that grading does not fulfill the four functions ascribed to it and that it can produce several undesirable motivational effects. In addition, the pressure on students to obtain good grades tends to undercut the purported beneficial effects of alternative marking approaches, when traditional and non-traditional methods coexist in the same system.

The research examining alternative approaches to grading suggests that finding satisfactory, workable alternatives will be difficult and may

[66] L. V. Ball. "Student Contracting for Achievement Grades in Ninth Grade General Mathematics." Doctoral dissertation. Storrs: University of Connecticut, 1973. Abstract available from Educational Resources Information Center, U.S. Office of Education: ED 081 623.

[67] W. L. Yarber. "Comparison of the Relationship of the Grade Contract and the Traditional Grading Methods to Changes in Knowledge and Attitude." *Journal of School Health* 44: 395-98; September 1974.

involve the restructuring of the whole curriculum around an individualized, competency-based or mastery-learning approach. In a recent article on alternatives to the present grading system, Van Hoven observed that:

> . . . we need a more scientific rationale for new directions in reporting pupil progress that reflect and are consistent with new approaches to the learning process. A non-competitive system of measuring a child's progress in achieving behavioral objectives is clearly defensible in the light of recent theories of intellectual growth and learning motivation research. Moreover, the actual programs developed as a result of these theories and studies do require new approaches to reporting pupil progress.[68]

Let us hope that future reviews of the research will report substantial progress toward a solution of the complex grading problem.

[68] J. B. Van Hoven. "Reporting Pupil Progress: A Broad Rationale for New Practices." *Phi Delta Kappan* 53: 365-66; February 1972.

An Overview of Grading Alternatives

James A. Bellanca and Howard Kirschenbaum

AT AN ANNUAL convention of the National Association of College Admissions Counselors, a portly white-haired high school counselor listened intently to a protracted and heated workshop debate on the merits of "traditional" and "non-traditional" grades. At the time the discussion became most heated, the counselor calmly took the floor. "I have worked with high school students," he began, "for more than three decades. In that time, I have seen and heard these arguments no less than seven times. What interests me the most about this particular discussion is the new definitions given the focal terms—'traditional' and 'non-traditional.' When my school was founded over a century ago, the traditional reporting method was a written letter sent home to the parents and a conference with each student once per month. Essentially, we use that same method today. What I want to point out here is the superficial misuse of these two key terms, which mean so little and yet receive so much attention. Let us put aside semantics and examine the real issues—*why do we have grades* and *why do we evaluate?*"

Just as the terms "traditional" and "non-traditional" do not help in answering these two important questions, so are the words "grades" and "evaluate" not likely to help, unless clearly defined.

Grading: Providing a numerical or letter symbol to summarize a student's progress or achievement within a given period of time

Reporting: Transmitting information about a student's progress or achievement to parents, employers, school records, or college admissions offices (transcripts, report cards, portfolios)

Evaluating: Making judgments regarding the quantity or quality of a student's progress or achievement

Measuring: Ascertaining the relative progress of a student as based on normative scales (for example, Iowa Reading Scale and Scholastic Aptitude Test norms)

These definitions point out the difficulties, inherent in each word, which have arisen through multiple use. Some school systems might use "grading" to mean an individual process distinct from "evaluating." Others use the term "grading" to encompass all four processes. Thus, when Sue Stone receives a report card, the A, B, A, C grades not only symbolize her progress for that semester, but also report the results from measuring devices (tests) used by her teachers to evaluate what they think Sue has learned.

Essentially, the definitions, as used in the implementation of a practical system, make clear two very distinct approaches to learning: normative and mastery. The vast majority of elementary, secondary, and college systems are norm-based. When teachers and students in a normative system speak of grades, they conceive of the processes of grading, evaluating, measuring, and reporting as one. Approximately one percent of college programs, on the other hand, use a mastery approach; slightly higher percentages of secondary and elementary systems have adopted mastery learning *in toto*, although as many as ten percent of the systems may use some form of mastery approach. Teachers and students who have implemented a mastery learning approach would distinguish each of the four processes listed above.

The Normative System

The normative system was introduced primarily as an efficient means to record the progress of large masses of students who appeared in urban schools after World War I. It later evolved into an approach to learning which measured a given student's performance in comparison to students who attended the same school or who took the same test. The norm is established by clustering scores of students along an imaginary line. Each cluster represents a standard of expected performance. For instance, a history teacher could determine that students whose answers were 95 percent correct had "outstanding" performance levels; 87 percent was "good"; 80 percent "average"; 72 percent "below average"; and below 72 percent was "failing work." An underlying assumption of the method is that most students taking the test would fall in the "average" group. A variation of the approach encourages the teacher to "average" the raw scores received by the students in the class. Thus, if answering 50 percent of the questions correctly is the "norm," then 50 percent would equal a C grade. Clusters emanating from the average would establish the other grades earned.

Although a statistician might quarrel with the validity of such a methodology, the two approaches described probably most closely represent the classroom practice of norm-based teachers. How well the system is used, however, is not the question. The crucial question should focus on the merits and demerits of the system itself.

Arguments For Norms

1. The normative system provides readily quantifiable information to establish grade point average (GPA) and rank in class (RIC). GPA and RIC provide colleges with the input used to determine college admissions. The 1971 joint review of RIC and GPA by the National Association of Secondary School Principals (NASSP) and the American Association of Collegiate Registrars and Admissions Officers (AACRAO) indicated that only 15.8 percent of those surveyed did *not* use one or both of these formulas.[1] Thirty-three and seven-tenths percent *required* RIC/GPA and 44.6 percent *requested* them from applicants. The committee that prepared this report recommended that: "secondary schools should continue to compute grade point averages as one element for use in the college application process" and that "secondary schools should provide rank in class for those colleges that require it as part of their admissions process." [2]

2. High school performance, as measured and reported through RIC, percentile rank, or GPA is the most reliable predictor of freshman college grades.[3]

3. The normative evaluation system is an integral component of the basic structure (Carnegie unit time schedule), content (departmental courses), and methodology of most secondary school programs.[4]

4. Life is competitive. The normative system, therefore, prepares students for the "real world." This system not only helps show the

[1] Warren Seyfert. "The Facts of the Case." *Bulletin of the National Association of Secondary School Principals* 56(365): 41-66; September 1972.

[2] Warren Seyfert and Committee. "Guidelines for Working with GPA and RIC." *Bulletin of the National Association of Secondary School Principals* 56(365): 62-82; September 1972.

[3] Jane Loeb. "High School Performance as Predictive of College Performance." *Bulletin of the National Association of Secondary School Principals* 56(365): 19-26; September 1972. This article gives an overview of significant research on this topic and provides an excellent bibliography; see also footnote references 4 and 5.

[4] Donald Hoyt. "The Relationship Between College Grades and Achievement." *ACT Research Paper No. 7.* Iowa City: American College Testing Program, 1965.

student the areas of future employment he or she should or should not consider, but also weeds out the chaff from the wheat.[5]

5. Admission to college is likewise competitive. The normative system provides an objective transcript which facilitates the fairest and most precise comparison of individual applicants. Grades reveal most succinctly the varying levels of achievement.[6]

6. Normative grades motivate students to study more diligently.[7]

7. Grades assist efficient record-keeping. Because of their easily quantified character, grades facilitate the teacher's obligatory report of a student's achievement to parents, future teachers, and future employers.[8]

8. Most scholarships and financial aid are dispensed on the basis of RIC and GPA.[9]

9. Most students prefer grades over non-traditional evaluations.[10]

Arguments Against Norms

1. Most colleges do review non-normative transcripts which do not provide GPA or RIC. The 1973 survey conducted for the *College Guide for Experimenting High Schools* reported that less than 5 percent of the respondents would *not* consider a transcript lacking RIC or GPA. Fifty-four percent indicated "fair and equal" review.[11]

[5] Howard Becker *et al. Making the Grade.* New York: John Wiley & Sons, Inc., 1958.

[6] R. L. Baker and R. F. Doyle. "A Change in Marking Procedures and Scholarship Achievement." *Educational Administration and Supervision,* Number 4; 1957. pp. 223-32.

[7] O. G. Brim *et al. The Use of Standardized Ability Tests in American Secondary Schools.* New York: Russell Sage Foundation, 1964. See also: R. A. Feldmesser. "The Positive Function of Grades." *Education Record;* Winter 1972. pp. 66-72.

[8] O. G. Brim *et al. A Survey: University and College Attitudes and Acceptance of Pass/Fail Courses.* Skokie, Illinois: National Association of College Admissions Counselors, 1972. See also: *Bulletin of the National Association of Secondary School Principals* 56(365); September 1972; and Max Marshall. *Teaching Without Grades.* Portland, Oregon: State University Press, 1969.

[9] Ruth Payne. "The Question of Financial Assistance." Mount Holyoke College *Alumnae Quarterly;* Spring 1973. pp. 10-14.

[10] Richard A. Gorton. "Comments on Research." *Bulletin of the National Association of Secondary School Principals* 56(365): 145-48; September 1972.

[11] James Bellanca and Howard Kirschenbaum. *College Guide for Experimenting High Schools.* Upper Jay, New York: National Humanistic Education Center, 1973.

2. Grades are, at most, a poor "predictor of success." The longer the time between the tests, the less the magnitude of correlation. The correlation between grades and long-range performance is moderate; that between grades and post-academic performance is practically nonexistent.[12]

3. Grades are the base for an academic system that has failed to achieve its own objectives. Grades promote superficial learning, poor teaching, and a "Watergate morality" in which ends justify means. "How to cheat or to con" is the major lesson mastered.[13]

4. Life in the 1970's demands that individuals and groups cooperate for survival. The 19th century survival-of-the-fittest philosophy is antithetical to the complex skills required to drive on a freeway, explore the moon, or solve modern economic problems.[14]

5. The college boom has peaked. Add the rising cost of a four-year college education to the lower number of potential applicants caused by the declining birthrate, and the reason that colleges have begun for the first time in many years to actively recruit candidates becomes clear.[15]

6. By definition, the normative system prevents the individualized and personalized learning which encourages each student to learn at the pace and by the means most suitable to her or him. Personalized learning, which encourages the intrinsic value of learning, is impossible when students perceive grades as their major goal.[16]

7. The normative system divides the learning community into divisive camps: Teachers are "obstacles" to be overcome; students are "pawns" to be manipulated.[17]

[12] Frank S. Jex. *Predicting Academic Success Beyond High School.* Salt Lake City, Utah: Institutional Studies Monograph, 1966.

[13] M. A. Fala. *Dunce Caps, Hickory Sticks, and Public Evaluations: The Structure of Academic Authoritarianism.* Madison, Wisconsin: The Teaching Assistant Association, University of Wisconsin, 1968.

[14] Douglas Looney. "Why Grab a Brass Ring?" *National Observer* 12(29): 1, 23; July 21, 1973.

[15] Clara Ludwig. "The Recruitment Riddle and Admissions Today." Mt. Holyoke College *Alumnae Quarterly;* Spring 1973. pp. 3-9.

[16] Arthur W. Combs. "Grading and How People Grow." In: *The National Conference on Grading Alternatives Workbook.* Cleveland, Ohio: National Humanistic Education Center, 1972.

[17] Sidney B. Simon. "Grading Must Go." *School Review* 78(3): 397-402; May 1970.

8. Grades are subjective, generally unscientific, and seldom related to established educational objectives. More often than not, grades establish a meritocracy that rewards conformity and compulsive compliance, and discourages individuality and creativity.[18]

In the 1960's when college students challenged the university establishment's use of grades as a competitive weapon, the pass-fail (P/F) syndrome developed. Although few colleges moved totally to the P/F system, many allowed students to elect P/F grades for nonacademic electives or other courses outside the "major." For the most part, P/F symbols became known as the non-traditional grades which eased, to a small degree, unnecessary academic competition.

Mastery Learning

When everyone's attention was focused on the arguments about pass-fail (P/F) and credit/no credit (C/NC) systems, little attention was given to the development of a different approach to learning—the mastery approach—then emanating from the theories of Benjamin Bloom. Mastery learning allows each student to proceed at his or her own pace with individually selected materials and methods in order to master the content, skills, and techniques which best satisfy his or her diagnosed needs and best prepare him or her to advance to more complex content, skills, and techniques. In this approach, evaluation becomes a key process involving the use of diagnostic and measurement tools to identify needs and provide helpful feedback. The reporting and recording processes are considered essential as administrative tools and are not considered as integral to learning.

When one discusses the mastery approach, it is quite easy to differentiate the various processes and define the functions of each. The majority of the favorable comments about mastery learning center on the classroom performance of and the positive learning behaviors exhibited by students who participate in good mastery programs. The negative comments center on the administrative processes of reporting and recording, processes which are less developed than the other aspects of this fledgling approach to learning.

In the mastery approach, there are three identifiable, but often overlapping methods of reporting and recording: the completion acknowledgment system, the criterion-referenced system, and the descriptive system. Each of these methods provides for a specific evaluation

[18] Howard Becker *et al. Making the Grade.* New York: John Wiley & Sons, Inc., 1968.

of a student's mastery learning and each possesses unique characteristics, both positive and negative.

Completion Acknowledgment System

The completion acknowledgment system reports that the student has completed the minimum requirements to earn credit for a course. The completion is reported in one of two ways: (a) course title, pass or credit symbol, and number of credits earned, or (b) course title, pass or credit symbol, number of credits earned or failure symbol, and no credit record. Some schools add variations such as honors (HonP), high pass (HP), and low pass (LP). No attempt is made to compare student performance or indicate course content. Schools using this system usually make no other major changes in organization, methodology, or content.

Symbols

P/F; Hon P/HP/LP/F; Credit/No Credit; Hon/P/No Record; U/S; HP/P/F; Pass/No Record; etc.

Arguments Pro

1. The completion acknowledgment system encourages students to explore, create, and investigate each subject.[19]

2. Competition is eliminated. The unnecessary anxiety of compulsive students and the damage to the self-image of less able students is minimized.[20]

3. Teachers learn to motivate students without reliance on the grade crutch.[21]

4. Students are free to decide which courses need the most attention. A student may decide to spend less time on a course that has little value for him or her, in order to concentrate his or her study on a course having a high personal priority.[22]

[19] William Glasser. *Schools Without Failure.* New York: Harper & Row, Publishers, 1969.

[20] Susan Wyatt. *The Mark: A Case for Abolition of Grading.* Washington, D.C.: Center for Educational Reform.

[21] W. L. Adams. "Why Teachers Say They Fail Pupils." *Educational Administration and Supervision,* Number 18; 1932. pp. 594-600.

[22] I. L. Child. "Determinants of Level of Aspiration: Evidence from Everyday Life." *Journal of Abnormal Psychology* 44(3): 303-14; 1949.

Arguments Contra

1. The completion acknowledgment system is more likely to hurt than to help. Although it removes the negative effect of the normative grades, it makes no attempt to correct the normative system's other weaknesses.[23]

2. This system provides the least assistance to those college admissions officers who need to distinguish degrees of ability and achievement. Without grades, GPA, RIC, or evaluative descriptions, the admissions officer must rely totally on standardized test scores. This procedure is unfair to all except the student who tests well. It also hinders scholarship and financial aid considerations, which are often based on a RIC test score formula.[24]

3. Most students, indoctrinated by the extrinsic motivations of the normative system, are not prepared for an overnight switch to the expectations of an intrinsic motivational system. Many students will react by working as little as possible for non-normative credit.[25]

4. This system does not provide the time or training for teachers to give evaluative feedback to the students.[26]

Criterion-Referenced System

The criterion-referenced system may use either the traditional or non-traditional grading symbols. It differs from the normative and completion acknowledgment systems in that it establishes a clear level of proficiency for each competency which the student is expected to master. A competency may be an individual skill or a concept in any of the three major domains: affective, cognitive, and psychomotor. Criterion-referenced systems are adaptable to group needs or individual instruction. "Contract" and "performance mastery" systems are based on criterion-referenced principles.

[23] Neil Postman. *What Is a Good School?* Upper Jay, New York: National Humanistic Education Center, 1972.

[24] Neil Postman. *A Survey: University and College Attitudes and Acceptance of High School Pass/Fail Courses.* Skokie, Illinois: National Association of College Admissions Counselors, 1972.

[25] Mathew Sgan. "Letter Grade Achievement in Pass/Fail Courses." *Journal of Higher Education* 41(8): 638-44; November 1970.

[26] George Bramer. "Grading and Academic Justice." *Improving College and University Teaching;* Winter 1970. pp. 63-65.

Symbols

A, B, C, D, No Record; P/NR; C/NC; S/U; etc., plus a listing of competencies mastered and/or a listing of criteria required for a passing or proficiency grade

Arguments Pro

1. The criterion-referenced system encourages individualized instruction. The teacher, working within the framework of clearly defined objectives, may devise, quite readily, different means to reach each objective. Individual students can work within personalized programs of instruction that meet specified learning needs in content, mode, and pace.[27]

2. This system removes the unnecessary pressure and anxiety of competitive grades by creating an atmosphere of cooperation. Teachers become helpers and peers provide support.[28]

3. Each student knows exactly what quantity and quality of work is expected.[29]

4. The criterion-referenced system focuses on success, not failure.[30]

5. Teachers are held accountable to establish clear objectives, develop a methodology that meets a variety of individual needs, and establish supportive evaluation tools.[31]

6. College admissions officers receive specific information about the skills each applicant has mastered and the knowledge he or she has. The facts are clearly delineated without need for subjective interpretation.[32]

[27] *The New High School: A School for Our Times.* New York: Committee on Experimentation, High School Division, April 1963.

[28] T. Strong, editor. *A Report of the Committee on the Freshman Year at California Institute of Technology.* Unpublished report. Pasadena, California: the Institute, 1967.

[29] Everett Shostrom. *Man the Manipulator.* New York: Bantam Books, Inc., 1968.

[30] John Holt. *How Children Fail.* New York: Dell Publishing Company, 1966.

[31] Leland Bradford. "The Teacher-Learning Transaction." *Adult Education* 8(3): 135-45; Spring 1958.

[32] Johannes Olson. "Initial Experiences of a No-Rank School." *Bulletin of the National Association of Secondary School Principals* 56(365): 103-104; September 1972.

Arguments Contra

1. The development of criteria, behavioral objectives, individualized learning packets, and other necessary instructional tools is in the infant stage. Objectives for achieving advanced skills and embracing more complex areas of knowledge, especially at the secondary level, are scarce. Hardware for individualized instruction is primitive and expensive; software is more so; and evaluative tools seem to be from the stone age. Most secondary schools do not possess the funds required for research, computer technology, staff development, and in-service training which the 5-point (A, B, C, D, NR) criterion-referenced system demands. The 2-point system (for example, C/NC) is somewhat easier to establish.[33]

2. The more detailed criterion-referenced systems tend to divide learning into isolated boxes. They ignore holistic patterns of human development, which call for the integration of feeling with knowledge.[34]

3. The criterion-referenced system overemphasizes quantity, response, performance, and preestablished norms in contrast to quality, self-initiated creativity, aesthetics, and discovery. (Again, this is less true the fewer the number of grading levels.)[35]

4. Most admissions officers do not have a clear set of admissions criteria which delineate minimum competencies expected of applicants at their schools.[36]

5. Although the criterion-referenced system is more objective than the normative and the descriptive evaluation systems, it generates more information than some admissions officers, pressured by time, will be able to process fairly.[37]

6. Without RIC and GPA, financial help may be jeopardized. (See completion acknowledgment.)

[33] Benjamin Bloom. "Learning for Mastery." *Evaluation Comment* of the University of California at Los Angeles, Center for the Study of Evaluation of Instructional Programs, Volume 1; May 1968.

[34] Carl Rogers. *Freedom To Learn.* Columbus, Ohio: Charles E. Merrill Publishing Company, 1969.

[35] John Holt. *How Children Learn.* New York: Dell Publishing Company, 1967.

[36] C. V. R. Halsey. "Comments on New Transcript Patterns." *Bulletin of the National Association of Secondary School Principals* 56(365): 118-31; September 1972.

[37] E. E. Oliver. "The New Guidelines." *Bulletin of the National Association of Secondary School Principals* 56(365): 83-88; September 1972.

Descriptive Evaluation System

The descriptive evaluation system details in written form the extent to which the content, skills, and/or techniques of each learning experience have been mastered in the context of the student's development as a person.

Symbols

None—uses written teacher evaluations and/or student self-evaluation

Arguments Pro

1. The descriptive system communicates the whole picture and not isolated learning blocks. This allows an admissions officer to judge capabilities, personality, and accomplishment on the basis of detailed information that creates an integrated and highly personalized picture of the applicant.[38]

2. The descriptive system allows for maximum flexibility for meeting individual needs in a very personalized manner. It is usually coupled with a whole definition of learning which encourages creativity, problem solving, personal growth, and the integration of knowledge with feeling. Learning, in this sense, begins with content and skills which are personally meaningful to the student and which reinforce a positive and realistic self-image based on success.[39]

3. A descriptive system focuses the student's attention on the processes by which he or she learns. "Process" receives equal ranking with "content" and with "product." Included in the process of learning-how-to-learn are learning-how-to-evaluate, learning-how-to-set-goals, and learning-how-to-plan-use-of-resources.[40]

4. Teachers and students must work closely together to prepare good evaluations. Cooperation places equal responsibility on students and teachers to build a climate of support, trust, and mutual respect.[41]

[38] *Report on Alternative School Transcripts.* Amherst, Massachusetts: National Alternative Schools Program, January 1973.

[39] William Purkey. *Self-Concept and School Achievement.* Englewood Cliffs, New Jersey: Prentice-Hall, Inc., 1970.

[40] Louise Berman. *New Priorities in the Curriculum.* Columbus, Ohio: Charles E. Merrill Publishing Company, 1968.

[41] Alfred Gorman. *Teachers and Learners: The Interactive Process in Education.* Boston: Allyn and Bacon, Inc., 1969.

Arguments Contra

1. Descriptive evaluations are too long and too complicated for some time-beleaguered admissions officers to read.[42]

2. An admissions officer is not concerned about personality. He needs to know if an individual can do college work.[43]

3. Descriptive evaluations sometimes tend to become subjective interpretations of achievement, usually described in vague generalities such as good, excellent, or fair.[44] Descriptive evaluations require skilled writers with the time and training to do the task in a manner fair to the student.[45]

4. Descriptive evaluations do not make or provide for comparisons by admissions officers.[46]

5. Descriptive evaluations could be a potent weapon against a student whom the teacher disliked.[47]

6. Without RIC or GPA, financial assistance may be jeopardized.[48]

---

[42] Alfred Gorman. Quoted in: *Grading and Reporting: Current Trends in School Policies & Programs*. Arlington, Virginia: National School Public Relations Association, 1972.

[43] Alfred Gorman. "Grading/Evaluation." In: *Memo to Faculty*. Ann Arbor, Michigan: University of Michigan, October 1971.

[44] C. Pascal. *Alternatives to Traditional Grading Procedures*. Unpublished manuscript. Montreal, Province of Quebec, Canada: McGill University, 1969.

[45] J. Karlins *et al.* "Academic Attitudes and Performance Functions of Differential Grading Systems: An Evaluation of Princeton's P/F System." *The Journal of Experimental Education* 37(3): 38-50; 1969.

[46] Allan Glatthorn. *Alternative Schools Project: Some Thoughts on Evaluation or Waddid-I-Get?* Upper Jay, New York: National Humanistic Education Center, 1972.

[47] Howard Kirschenbaum, Sidney B. Simon, and Rodney W. Napier. *Wad-Ja-Get? The Grading Game in American Education*. New York: Hart Publishing Company, Inc., 1971.

[48] Joseph Vander Zanden. "One District's Efforts To Remove Rank in Class." *Bulletin of the National Association of Secondary School Principals* 56(365): 89-95; September 1972.

Part III

Some Alternatives
That Work

THERE MAY BE no more difficult reform task than introducing a non-grade report system into schools. Everyone wants it, but few initiate it! In this section are articles which describe innovative alternatives that: (a) have worked; (b) have been accepted; and (c) have lasted. They range from a contract system for college students to a computerized criterion-referenced system for levels K through 8.

A Computerized Alternative To Grading

Keith V. Burba

SOMETHING WAS WRONG. Communication between community and school desperately needed revamping.

The need to establish better communication patterns became apparent at a human relations conference involving teachers and administrators in the Beecher School District, Flint, Michigan.

Teachers and principals from three particular schools in the district decided to take action on these needs. All three schools decided that a new system of reporting from school to parents was in order. This was a big step from the traditional A, B, C, D, E that had been uniformly used throughout the district. One of the schools, Harrow Elementary, planned an additional change: an individualized instruction organization for every grade level in the K-6 building.

Analyzing Substance of Reports

Teachers began to meet informally to discuss which method of reporting they preferred. Also, teachers began compiling lists of skills, concepts, and attitudes they wanted to share with parents. At this point, parents from the community were asked what types of information they would like to have from the school.

From this informal setting, a reporting committee emerged comprised of teachers from each grade level (K-6), parents, and administrators.

Each area of the curriculum was considered in depth. Reporting on student conduct and attitudes was of particular concern to the committee, although grades in conduct seemed irrelevant and ambiguous. The group felt that parents should be informed about the behavior patterns of their children, as well as their academic progress. Attitudes and values which students exhibit toward school in general, and toward pupil-teacher and peer relationships were seen as being directly related to the learning process. It was felt that meaningful dialogue in this area could encourage better school-community relations.

Describing Teacher Comments

After the attitude and conduct area was studied, each of the subject areas was considered. All skills and concepts taught at each grade level in all of the academic disciplines were compiled. As one can imagine, the committee had many pages of comments.

For each skill or concept taught, the committee felt there were four ways to report student progress to parents. Comments might be descriptive, prescriptive, positive, or negative as illustrated by the following examples.

Descriptive
- Understands the concepts of left and right
- Prints own name

Prescriptive
- Needs more work in adding two-digit numbers
- Needs to be encouraged to read for pleasure

Positive
- Able to recognize a verb
- Shows an interest in nature

Negative
- Lacks self-control
- Not reading up to grade level orally

Choosing a New Method of Reporting

After they had determined specific types of information that they wanted to use in communicating to parents, the committee members then had to develop a method to report this information most efficiently. Some of the reporting alternatives studied were: (a) handwritten evaluations from teacher to parent; (b) check lists; (c) modified handwritten check lists; and (d) use of a computer.

The strengths and weaknesses of the first three reporting alternatives mentioned above were studied and those methods discarded. The committee then decided to explore the possibility of a computerized reporting system.

Since child accounting and high school reporting for Beecher schools were already handled by computer (through the Genesee County Intermediate School District), experienced personnel were asked if they could help develop a computerized narrative reporting system. Billie D. White, director of data processing, developed a program to produce the desired reporting mechanism: narrative statements in paragraph form.

Since the computer's total capacity was 9,999 comments, over 1,000 narrative possibilities existed for each of the nine educational parameters (listed in categories below) on which teachers would be reporting.

1000 Attitude and Conduct	*6000 Health*
2000 Language Arts	*7000 Physical Education*
3000 Math	*8000 Art*
4000 Social Studies	*9000 Music*
5000 Science	

Narrative statements were grouped within each of these nine categories to form the narrative catalogue; each statement was assigned a four-digit identification number from the numbers available to its category. All narrative statements had to be limited to 72 characters. The final catalogue, which included over 1,100 comments, represented less than one-tenth of the capacity of the total computer system.

Using Computerized Reporting

At the end of a marking period, teachers now receive a catalogue of narratives (as described above) and a student worksheet for each pupil. On the worksheet is the student's name, teacher's name, date, and categories beginning with *1000 Attitude and Conduct* and going through *9000 Music*. After each of the nine categories are 15 blanks. The teacher can choose up to 15 comments for any one of the categories. In total, the teacher can use 56 comments to describe the progress of the student during the marking period. In short, the teacher writes in the appropriate four-digit numbers, and the computer prints out the corresponding statements. It takes data processing one week to keypunch the numbers assigned to the narratives and to run the cards through the computer.

The descriptive narrative report for each student comes back from data processing in paragraph form, sectioned off into the nine major categories. The school receives three copies of each report. Copies go to teacher and parents, and are put with cumulative records.

Also, a usage report is supplied which tells how many times each comment was used for a marking period. This has been helpful in determining which narratives are not needed. Also, the usage report gives some insight into what is being taught in the classroom. The system can be up-dated each marking period.

Cost for the program is $.20 per child per marking period, or $.80 per child per year.

Advantages of New System

In an effort to close the communication gap in changing to a new reporting system, the staff felt it important to conduct parent-teacher conferences. The first conferences seemed so well received that teachers decided to use this method twice each year.

Following are some of the specific advantages and strengths of the narrative reporting system.

1. *Effective Utilization of Computerization:* The data processing system developed tends to produce a more comprehensive narrative report because of the computer's storage capacity of 9,999 comments. This helps the teacher to avoid using generalizing clichés or educational jargon concerning the student's behavior and achievement. Also, since the printout is organized in paragraph form, the parent can more easily understand what the teacher is communicating.

2. *Flexibility of System:* Narratives can be added to or deleted from the system at any time. Because of its capacity, the system can be changed by merely assigning a new narrative to an available four-digit number within a given category. Also, the total usage report (explained earlier) can be used as a yardstick to make the system more efficient. If a narrative is not being used by the staff, it may easily be deleted.

3. *More Realistic Than Grades:* Each narrative relates directly to some skill, concept, or attitude contributing to the teaching-learning act during a reporting period. In other words, rather than assign a student a grade of C in *Language Arts*, the teacher can share with the parents the specific skills their child was exposed to during the evaluation period which he or she did or did not develop. In addition to this information, the teacher can suggest the skills in which the student needs further work.

4. *More Thorough Evaluation:* The system demands that the teacher make a more thorough cumulative evaluation of the student. Instead of recording mere grades in the traditional grade book, teachers must keep track of a student's progress in each skill or concept to which he or she has been exposed during a marking period. Also, the teacher is spared the

Computerized Narrative Reporting System
Beecher School District, Flint, Michigan
From the Narrative Comment Catalog—Category: 5000 Science

Number	Teacher Comment
5856	Needs Further Work Identifying Three-Dimensional Objects
5861	Understands Addition of One-Digit Numerals
5866	Needs Further Work Understanding the Addition of One-Digit Numerals
5871	Can Identify Angles
5876	Needs Further Work Identifying Angles
5881	Can Identify Short Periods of Time
5886	Needs Further Work in Identifying Short Periods of Time
5891	Can Identify the Area of Figures
5896	Needs Further Work in Identifying the Area of Figures
5901	Can Identify the Color, Shape, and Size of Objects
5906	Needs Further Work in Identifying the Color, Shape, and Size of Objects
5911	Can Identify Physical Changes in an Object
5916	Needs Further Work in Identifying Physical Changes in an Object
5921	Can Identify Objects by Weight
5926	Needs Further Work in Identifying Objects by Weight
5931	Can Identify Changes in a Plant
5936	Needs Further Work Identifying Changes in a Plant
5941	Can Identify the Increase in Size of Seeds Soaked in Water
5946	Needs Work Identifying the Increase in Size of Seeds Soaked in Water
5951	Has Successfully Completed a Reptile Unit
5953	Has Successfully Completed a Bird Unit
5955	Has Successfully Completed a Mammal Unit
5957	Has Successfully Completed an Insect Unit
5959	Has Not Successfully Completed a Reptile Unit
5961	Has Not Successfully Completed a Bird Unit
5963	Has Not Successfully Completed a Mammal Unit
5965	Has Not Successfully Completed an Insect Unit
5967	Is Able To Name and Identify the 6 Simple Machines
5969	Needs More Study To Be Able to Name and Identify 6 Simple Machines
5971	Does Not Know the 6 Simple Machines
5973	Understands the Term Friction
5975	Needs More Study To Be Able to Understand the Word Friction
5977	Does Not Understand the Term Friction
5979	Knows Terms Related to Study of Simple Machine, e.g., Force-Resistance

tasks of deciding what constitutes an A on one end of the spectrum, and an F on the other end or how to flunk a child of a low-achieving status without stifling a desire to learn.

5. *Improving Learning Environment Within the Classroom:* Several teachers have said that the system not only forced them to look more closely at each child, but also caused them to look more closely at the teaching act. Because it fosters careful scrutiny, computerized narrative reporting has proven to be a means of upgrading instruction. In addition, when a child changes teachers at the end of a school year, his or her new teachers can see specifically what skills or concepts the student has mastered previously and can thus develop accordingly a continuing individualized program for that child.

6. *Discourages Unfavorable Comparisons:* Because each report is individualized and *narratives* are used to report to parents, the system tends to cause parents to look at their child's report using the child's particular frame of reference. Thus, it becomes less likely that parents will punish children for poor grades or compare them negatively with other children.

Need was seen at Harrow Elementary School, Beecher School District, Flint, Michigan, for a revised reporting system. A computerized narrative reporting system was developed because of its several advantages. These include the effectiveness of computerization, coupled with the system's flexibility, realistic application, and thoroughness. Other major advantages of the system are that it tends to improve the learning environment within the classroom and to discourage unfavorable comparisons of siblings by parents.

A Contract Method of Evaluation

Arthur W. Combs

THE METHOD OF grading now used in my teaching is the product of 15 years of trial and error. It is the best method I have found to date for meeting the following essential criteria:

A desirable grading system should:

- Meet college and university standards of effort, performance, and excellence;
- Evaluate the student on his or her personal performance rather than in competition with his or her fellow students;
- Permit students to work for whatever goal they desire to shoot for;
- Provide the broadest possible field of choice for each student;
- Challenge students to stretch themselves to their utmost;
- Eliminate as much as possible all sources of externally imposed threat;
- Involve the student actively in planning for personal learning and placing the responsibility for this learning directly and unequivocally on the student's own shoulders;
- Free the student as much as possible from the necessity of pleasing the instructor;
- Provide maximum flexibility to meet changing conditions.

To meet these criteria my current practice is to enter into a contract with each student for the grade he or she would like to achieve. Each student writes a contract with the instructor indicating in great detail: (a) the grade he or she would like to have; (b) what he or she proposes to do to achieve it; and (c) how he or she proposes to demonstrate that he or she has achieved it. Once this contract has been signed by the student and instructor, the student is, thereafter, free to move in any way desired to complete the contract. When the contract has been completed "in letter and in spirit" the student's grade is automatic.

Beginning the Negotiations

At the second meeting of the class the philosophy and procedures for this method of evaluation are carefully explained. Students are given two blank contracts on which to file proposals in duplicate, and a deadline date (usually one-fourth to one-third of the way through the semester) is set at which time all contracts must be in and approved. The student is told that in proposing the contract two things need to be taken into consideration: (a) what the student would like to do, and (b) what the university has a right to expect of a person working for that grade.

Next, the instructor discusses with the student: (a) the general criteria for grades in the college, and (b) the specific ways in which these criteria may be met in this particular class. While these criteria, of course, differ from class to class, they fall generally within this framework: For a grade of C, the college requires satisfactory completion of the basic requirements of the course. My requirements are spelled out in detail for a particular course including such things as attendance at all class meetings, required and optional readings, and other specifics which I intend to require of all students throughout the semester. These latter might be written reports, projects, observations, participation in research, and additional assignments.

For a grade of B, the college requires completion of all of the basic requirements for the course, plus an additional program of study above and beyond that generally expected of all students. This is interpreted for my classes to mean that a student may propose: (a) some special area of intensive study, or (b) a research or action project of merit.

For a grade of A, the college requires satisfactory completion of the requirements for C and B levels, plus the consistent demonstration of a high level of scholarship, interest, and excellence in the subject matter of the course. For my classes this is interpreted to mean that students working for an A must satisfactorily complete work at the B and C levels and take a stiff essay examination. The contract blank provides space for students to write side-by-side both what is proposed for a particular grade and how they propose to demonstrate completion of that proposal.

Contracts must be written out in great detail, indicating precisely what is to be done and how, at every step of the way. Care is taken to assure that a student gives a good deal of thought to the contract at the time it is filed to make certain that no misunderstanding occurs at the end of the semester, when the decision must be made about whether the contract has been fulfilled.

A long period for planning contracts is purposely allocated to provide students with enough time to: (a) get a feel for the course and, (b) make preliminary explorations of problems they might like to tackle in special study or special projects. As soon as a student has made out the contract, it is submitted in duplicate to the instructor, who may suggest additions, deletions, or modifications of one sort or another during a discussion period. Once the contract has been signed by the instructor, there are no examinations in the course except the one selected by students working for A grades.

During the semester, if it becomes necessary for students to make a change in their contracts, they may do so by requesting renegotiation after which appropriate modifications will be made. There is one exception to this: Contracts may be modified at the same level or a lesser level but a student, once having decided to work for a particular grade, may not decide to work for a higher one. After all, a student who is going to work for a superior grade must begin this process at the very start of the semester.

The method of demonstration by which the student will show completion of the contract is the student's choice. Students may put on a demonstration for the class, write a paper, run an experiment, do a tape recording, keep a log of personal experiences, or whatever seems appropriate.

If a student does not complete the grade contracted for, then the grade automatically drops to the highest previous level satisfactorily completed. Thus, a person who contracted for an A grade but decided not to take the final examination would automatically receive a B grade if all the work is complete at that level. Similarly, a student working for a C grade, who "fudged" on the basic requirements of the course, would move back to a D grade or even to an F grade depending upon the degree of dereliction.

Students React Favorably

While this system of evaluation is by no means perfect, it has proven far more satisfactory than the traditional methods of grading and evaluation I formerly used. Students are sometimes upset by the procedure at first and may object to having so much responsibility placed upon them. These objections, however, quickly dissipate as the student discovers a brand new freedom which even permits disagreement with the instructor with impunity. Experience has shown that students read far more under this system, work much harder, and show far more originality, spontaneity, and creativity. The response of the students has mostly been enthusiastically favorable. From the instructor's view, it has proven eminently satisfactory. The technique is not foolproof, however, and occasionally a student misuses privileges. But as one of my students expressed it, "I guess you know that sometimes students take advantage of your grading system—but then, I guess the old system took advantage of the student!"

A Case Study: Performance Evaluation at Concord Senior High School

*William J. Bailey**

THE PROPER EVALUATION of student progress is obviously one of the most important activities of schools; yet traditionally, evaluation procedures have been perhaps the most abused of all practices in the schools.

There are many ways in which schools provide an atmosphere of failing, but the traditional system of arbitrarily placing students in one of five categories (A, B, C, D, F) is the most damaging of all. The most injurious category, that of failure (D or F), asks the student to place himself or herself in the hands of the teacher for rewards based not on *what* he or she learned, but on whether others learned more. If we translate letter grades into traditional numerical standards, we can have one student attaining 69 and failing, while another attains 70 and passes, with no allowances being made for time differentials in learning. There are only two grades (A or B) about which students feel good or feel any sense of worth.

It is a punitive system indeed which categorizes participants so that only the few are successful. In addition, studies have shown that there are many discrepancies, inaccuracies, and biases present in the decision-making process of assigning students one of the normal five grades.[1] This is due to the generally vague criteria involved in grading—criteria which vary in types of components and in the relative weight given to

* A former principal describes grading reform initiated during his administration.

[1] Howard Kirschenbaum, Sidney B. Simon, and Rodney W. Napier. *Wad-Ja-Get? The Grading Game in American Education.* New York: Hart Publishing Company, Inc., 1971.

discipline, attitude, skills, attendance, subject matter competency, and other factors.

Failure is structured into the American system of public education. Losers are essential to the success of the winners. Concord High School in Wilmington, Delaware, was determined to change that structure.

Present System: Conflict and Frustration

The present grading situation is partially a result of an inherent sociological conflict between two views. On the one hand, society has historically presented education-beyond-the-minimal as something for the select few. On the other hand, modern society now contends that advanced forms of education must be made available for all. School learning has become necessary for the many. The economic potential of this nation offers possibilities unlimited to those with the proper education, career choice, and job performance skills. There is no longer a need to discourage a certain faction of the society from furthering its education and training because of poor grades. However, much of our present educational system is doing just that because of the frustration facing the majority of young students.

Part of this frustration is due to the traditional norm-based grading system in which only one-third of the students are successful (A and B students). The source of this conflict educationally is the normal curve. Benjamin Bloom speaks to the point beautifully.

> We have for so long used the normal curve in grading students that we have come to believe in it. . . . There is nothing sacred about the normal curve. It is the distribution most appropriate to chance and random activity. Education is a purposeful activity and we seek to have the students learn what we have to teach. If we are effective in our instruction, the distribution of achievement should be very different from the normal curve. In fact, we may even insist that our education efforts have been unsuccessful to the extent to which our distribution of achievement approximates the normal distribution.[2]

College admission practices can adjust to whatever system the secondary schools offer if there is sufficient information available about students.

It is significant that a survey conducted by Purdue University [3]

[2] Benjamin S. Bloom. "Learning for Mastery." *Evaluation Comment* of the University of California at Los Angeles, Center for the Study of Evaluation of Instructional Programs, Volume 1; May 1968.

[3] A. C. Erlich. *High Schools in 1970: A Study of the Student-School Relationship.* West Lafayette, Indiana: Purdue University Measurement and Research Center, 1970.

revealed that 40 percent of high school students found their schools "repressive" and considered education an "assembly line process." It is also significant that our nation faces many social problems such as increases in mental illness, unemployment, divorce rate, drug abuse, violence, and general social and political instability. We must provide for schools in which our future citizens can develop positive mental attitudes, high self-concepts, and a sense of vocational direction, and in which they can establish a success pattern through a reasonable use of their capacities. If we cannot do that, we will do little to solve the major problems of the nation.

If we want schools to be significantly better, then they must be significantly different. A change in the evaluation system is long overdue. Concord High School tried to make this change during the time that I was principal.

A Partial Solution

If schools are to develop their own philosophy, then their evaluation system must enhance that philosophy. The new system for Concord placed emphasis on the individual learner, de-emphasized time as a limitation to learning, and stressed the importance of precise objectives in dealing with specific criteria used in evaluation.

The new system was designed to increase the accountability and reliability of our educational endeavors. This was possible through increased objectivity in evaluating student progress; improved diagnostic competency-procedures effected upon student entry into a course; established behavioral and criterion-based objectives for each course; measured observable performances and actual growth; and improved teaching methods, which allowed for individualized and continuous progress learning. There were two major parts of the Concord evaluation process: (a) formative, and (b) summative.

Formative Evaluation

First, an interim progress reporting procedure dealing with *formative* evaluations was adopted. Frequent formative evaluation tests and other appraisals provided an indication of the pace and motivation of the students. They also indicated if the student were making the necessary effort at the appropriate time. The appropriate use of these evaluations helped to ensure that each set of learning tasks was sufficiently learned before subsequent learning tasks were started. A check was made every nine weeks or less and the results were forwarded to parents.

Each department was responsible for developing its own formative evaluations and the necessary forms. These evaluation forms utilized the summative coding system symbols for report card usage and included a one- or two-page supplementary progress report, which gave a specific recording of subject matter learned, student attitude, and other information pertinent to the uniqueness of the individual course.

Summative Evaluation

The other part of the evaluation system involved the final recording of achievement referred to as the summative evaluation. The summative evaluation was a summary of the work for the entire course, a recording of student achievement level that included a coding system for college transcripts, and general pertinent comments regarding the individual student, along with recommendations for future work in the areas noted. (See examples on following pages.)

The summative evaluation was designed to award credit for achievement on two levels, plus an additional accomplishment/service category that was highly selective. The basic achievement level, called "sufficient," denoted that the student had achieved or acquired the necessary skills, concepts, or attitudes that met course standards. This sufficiency level was available to and attainable by all students in Concord High School given proper placement and normal time allotments, although some took longer than others to achieve sufficiency.

The "proficient" level signified a demonstration of unusual interest, motivation, skills, knowledge, or advanced concepts. It was available to and attainable by 90 percent of the students at Concord given: (a) the appropriate mode of instruction (materials and teacher), (b) unlimited time, and (c) adequate motivation. Since many students were not able to hurdle these givens, the proficiency level was somewhat discriminating.

The third category was an arrangement starting after or along with the proficiency achievement level, but requiring additionally that the student enter into a contract to be of service to the discipline. This "master status" was limited to one course per student per year. Examples of possible master service included: (a) acting as student aide to a teacher; (b) assisting in a laboratory; (c) tutoring; (d) researching special projects; (e) writing learning packets/producing audio-visual aids; and (f) engaging in certain kinds of individual study.

It was important to consider all three achievement levels in the light of a transition from a system involving student comparisons, toward an achievement system in which the student competed against the course.

Performance Evaluation—Concord High School
Wilmington, Delaware
Analysis of major literary elements (Huck Finn)—Phase III

Character Objective: The student will analyze in depth the characters of Huck, Jim, and Tom—designating their distinctive qualities, their similarities, and their differences.

Task:

(1) The student will write one paragraph each, supporting a major trait of Huck and Jim (a total of two paragraphs).

(2) The student will write one paragraph of comparison/contrast supporting a point of similarity or difference between Huck and Tom; and

(3) The student will write a multi-paragraph paper tracing the stages in the development of Huck's character.

Criteria:

Proficiency—valid and insightful hypothesis supported by ample and well chosen evidence.

Sufficiency—valid hypothesis supported by scant and/or poorly chosen evidence.

No Credit—invalid hypothesis and/or insufficient support.

Setting Objective: The student will analyze the significance of setting, including larger areas and details within descriptions.

Task:

(1) Given a passage, the student will list significant details and, in one sentence, state their significance; and

(2) The student will write in class one paragraph developed by comparison/contrast stating the significance of the shore and the river. He or she will use at least three specific episodes in each setting to support his or her position.

Criteria: Passage

Proficiency: 9 to 10 well chosen and supported details.
Sufficiency: 6 to 8 well chosen and supported details.
No Credit: 0 to 5.

Criteria: Paragraph

Proficiency: Clear basis for contrast and full use of supporting episodes.
Sufficiency: Clear basis for contrast but weaker support.
No Credit: Lack of basis for contrast and/or failure to provide sufficient support.

Performance Evaluation—Concord High School
Wilmington, Delaware
Chemistry/Physics—Interim Report

Student	**Date**

Levels of Student Operation

S—Sufficiency—Performance of basic skills and understanding of basic concepts.

P—Proficiency—Performance of advanced skills, understanding of advanced concepts, and/or in-depth study.

NC—No Credit—Performance below sufficiency requirements.

I—Incomplete—Required tasks in progress to be evaluated at a later date.

M—Mastery—A final grade only. Performance at proficiency level, plus consistent application of advanced skills and concepts.

Student Progress

Student is working at _____ level.

Content Areas	Topic Complete	Working on Topic but Not Complete	Topic Not Started	Student Should Be on This Topic To Be on Schedule
1. Communications				
2. Measurement				
3. Kinematics				
4. Dynamics				
5. Motion in the Heavens				
6. Conservation Laws				
7. Kinetic Theory of Gases				
8. Basic Chemical Principles				

Lab reports: _____ No. complete _____ No. incomplete

	Poor	Fair	Good
Work Habits			
Attitude			
Utilization of time			

Teacher comments:

Parent comments are invited on reverse side of report.

Parent Signature

Providing Meaningful Information

The traditional transcript format was used for college admission purposes. The symbols for the coding system (NC, S, P, M) were entered as were grades in the past. Each student had on file the summative evaluation form for each course completed. The back of the form contained a description of the course and specific achievements made by the student in relation to the course; *formats varied with the department.*

When advisable, these forms were included with college or job applications. If necessary all of the summative evaluations were sent to interested parties; however, it was more probable that only those specifically pertaining to the student's major interest would be necessary. For example, a student with primary interests in engineering might send the math and science reports. Of course, transcripts still contained the regular test scores and faculty recommendations, but they included no grade point average or class rank.

Summary

The change at Concord required input from many sources; all of the following contributed to the decision-making process.

1. *Concord Curriculum Board:* This body was the curriculum decision-making group of Concord High School. The board consisted of students, teachers, counselors, and supervisory personnel—all of whom were involved in assessing the school's educational practices. The curriculum board gave its express permission to the undertaking of the proposed grading change.

2. *Concord Student Cabinet:* This group of students controlled student activities and influenced school-wide decisions. The cabinet supported the movement.

3. *Concord Citizens' Advisory Committee:* This was a lay group of parents, students, and citizens who jointly served as a liaison between the school, the community, and the school board. They showed unusual interest in the project.

4. *Alfred I. du Pont Curriculum Council:* Members of this group, experienced and well known educators in the district, made recommendations of a curricular nature to the superintendent and board of education. They were closely involved with Concord's instructional strategies and they gave their approval to the new evaluation system.

5. *Concord PTA:* The PTA made presentations to explain the new system and help solve public relations problems.

The carefully planned change in the Concord evaluation system was successful. It was initiated, implemented, and operational. However, following the successful implementation of the new system, a change in administration took place. This change in administration at the local building and at the district office resulted in a gradual revision of the evaluation process to a more traditional system.

Changes involving a move toward traditionalism were evident in other areas also, shifts that seem to be typical of the history of innovative schools when the administrator/change agent leaves. However, the significant insight provided by the Concord case study is that real change can be made. Changes in the grading system can be made in other schools as well, as long as the administrative leadership is forthright.

References

H. Becker, B. Grier, and E. Hughes. *Making the Grade: The Academic Side of College Life.* New York: John Wiley & Sons, 1968.

John Bevan, editor. *AACRAO Survey on College Grading Systems.* Unpublished report. Washington, D.C.: American Association of Collegiate Registrars and Admissions Officers, 1971.

Benjamin S. Bloom. "Learning for Mastery." *Evaluation Comment* of the University of California at Los Angeles, Center for the Study of Evaluation of Instructional Programs, Volume 1; May 1968.

Benjamin S. Bloom, J. Thomas Hastings, and George F. Madaus. *Handbook on Formative and Summative Evaluation of Student Learning.* New York: McGraw-Hill Book Company, 1971.

Robert M. Gagné. *The Conditions of Learning.* New York: Holt, Rinehart and Winston, 1965.

William Glasser. *Schools Without Failure.* New York: Harper & Row, Publishers, 1969.

J. McV. Hunt. *Intelligence and Experience.* New York: The Ronald Press Company, 1961.

Howard Kirschenbaum, Sidney B. Simon, and Rodney W. Napier. *Wad-Ja-Get? The Grading Game in American Education.* New York: Hart Publishing Company, Inc., 1971.

Robert F. Mager. *Developing Attitudes Toward Learning.* Palo Alto, California: Fearon Publishers, 1968.

Ellis P. Page. "Teacher Comments and Student Performance." In: W. W. Charters, Jr., and N. L. Gage, editors. *Readings in the Social Psychology of Education.* Boston: Allyn and Bacon, Inc., 1963.

Sidney P. Rollins. *Developing Nongraded Schools.* Itasca, Illinois: F. E. Peacock Publishers, Inc., 1968.

Arlene Silberman. "Are Marks Really Necessary?" *Seventeen Magazine;* May 1971. pp. 154-99.

Charles E. Silberman. *Crisis in the Classroom.* New York: Random House, Inc., 1970.

James S. Terwilliger. "Marking Practices and Policies in Public Secondary Schools." *Bulletin of the National Association of Secondary School Principals* 50(308): 5-37; March 1966.

Fred T. Wilhelms, editor. *Evaluation as Feedback and Guide.* Washington, D.C.: Association for Supervision and Curriculum Development, 1967.

New Reports for New Schooling at John Adams High School

Donald D. Holt

HOW CAN A school staff allow for a wider range of learning experiences than is usually open to high school students? How can a school staff eliminate, through choice, the negative effects of grading? In order to answer these two questions, John Adams High School in Portland, Oregon, developed a two-track grading system: the student's choice of traditional grades or of P/F with written evaluation.[1]

Credit may be given for any course listed in John Adams High School's curriculum after the student has met the minimum performance and attendance qualifications that were established for the course by the certificated person of record. Students may receive credit if they are properly enrolled through the data processing and programming procedures that are part of each school and the instructional division.

Students are eligible to receive credit when the following have been accomplished by the person of record:

1. The person of record will complete the course description form that includes title, course description, total weeks of instruction, and amount of credit for the course;

2. This statement must be approved by the school director who will submit it to the vice principal in the instructional division for authorization or rejection;

[1] *Schools-Within-a-School.* John Adams High School Operational Handbook. Portland, Oregon: John Adams High School, 1975.

3. Once authorized, the instructional division will arrange for scheduling and will credit authorization with data processing;

4. A student will then be considered enrolled in the class;

5. Credit will not be allowed for student experiences that have not been cleared in advance by the procedures described above.

Learning experiences at John Adams fall into three categories: (a) experience courses of an intern or apprentice nature; (b) off-campus learning experiences; and (c) on-campus courses.

Experience Courses: Credit is to be given to student secretaries, student assistants, and/or student aides only when their evaluation forms are signed/authorized by a certificated staff member. The evaluation must include the total number of periods comprising the student experience. Any instruction by non-certificated personnel must be under the direction and control of a certificated person, who serves as teacher of record and assumes responsibility for the instruction and the results.

Off-Campus Learning Experience: In order to receive credit a student must prepare an experience contract and submit it to the school director who will have it placed on file with the instructional division *prior* to commencement of the experience. The school director will authorize the transcript secretary to record credit for the experience after an evaluation has been received from the community sponsor.

Course Designations: It is the responsibility of the school director to designate and code each course intended to satisfy course work required by the State of Oregon and by the school district for graduation. John Adams uses the following codes preceding course title when submitting course statements for authorization.

Code	Requirement To Be Satisfied	Code	Requirement To Be Satisfied
E/C	*English/Communication*	S	*Science*
SS	*Social Science*	LS	*Laboratory Science* *
	(also American	PF	*Personal Finance* *
	Problems)	CE	*Career Education* *
US	*U.S. History*	PE	*Physical Education*
Cit	*Citizenship* *	H	*Health*
M	*Mathematics*	DE	*Driver Education*

  * *Class of '78 and after.*

All evaluation forms that may be part of the credit-granting system (for example, report cards and data processing reports) must indicate attendance in terms of the total number of periods of participation for the amount of credit granted.

All classes should be accounted for in record books by course instructors; each instructor will record the attendance of every student enrolled in his or her course. At the completion of the course, the record books are turned in to the instructional division. They serve as the final source on any student's enrollment. The record book must show the total number of periods of participation and amount of credit awarded.

The circumstance in which No Credit is given to a student during a reporting period can be changed by a teacher after the student has met the course requirements of the instructor. The authority to change the No-Credit status is limited to the teacher of record for the course. Note that the eligibility rules of the Oregon School Activity Association require that: "A student shall have been in regular attendance, enrolled in and doing passing work in four (4) full and regular subjects at the close of the preceding semester as well as the current semester. . . . No student shall be permitted to make up any eligibility deficiency in scholarship after the semester ends." This means that students must have passed four courses during the last semester in order to be eligible. It also means that credit cannot be made up for eligibility after a semester ends.

All students at John Adams High School have the option of receiving evaluation in courses either in the form of a grade (A, B, C, or No Pass) or in the form of Pass or No Pass. A student is automatically enrolled on a Pass/No Pass basis unless the teacher is notified to enroll the student for letter grades. The decision to opt for letter grades can be made by either students or parents.

Students who elect to take a Pass/No Pass evaluation will receive a written evaluation of their progress. Students who elect to take grades (A, B, C) will receive a written evaluation at the discretion of the teacher. In all cases where a student receives a No Pass, the evaluation will automatically be supported by a written comment. It is recommended, in cases where a student receives a No Pass, that the conditions needed to receive a passing evaluation be identified by the teacher.

Written evaluations are to include course information, counselor's name, written comments, the grade and/or the amount of credit awarded or restored, and the number of days absent during the quarter. The written comments are to provide personalized and descriptive information for the student and parent.

Each teacher prepares complete reports which describe specific course expectations, as well as the student's individual progress. The teachers receive one full day's release time at the end of each quarter to write evaluations.

Data processing printouts of student grades/credits/attendance are part of the Adams records. The vice principal in the instructional division (IS/MD) establishes and interprets staff procedure for organizing grade, credit, and attendance information for data processing.

The teacher of record has sole responsibility for the preparation of written evaluations and the organization of information for data processing. The teacher must have supportive records of student work and attendance.

School directors are responsible for interpreting evaluation policies to their staff members, as well as for consulting the staff regarding the preparation of student evaluations and data processing information.

The head of the IS/MD and the school directors are responsible for interpreting and enforcing school policy regarding student evaluations.

The student or parent may challenge the teacher's adherence to school policy on the accuracy or completeness of the records. Such a challenge must first be made directly to the teacher of record. Subsequent resolution can be sought through the school director and the IS/MD vice principal.

Students have the option of preparing a written evaluation of their own progress in any course, to be used in addition to the teacher's comments. These evaluations are included in all records and mailings.

The official school district transcript of each student's records is maintained by the transcript/records secretary of the administrative division. The secretary also prepares unofficial copies of transcripts for all students and for counseling and programming purposes. Coordinating and maintaining the accuracy of information for all transcript entries are the responsibilities of each school director. Correction of official records is made according to mark up-date forms submitted to the records office by the teacher of record.

Records are altered only by the records secretary, based on the school director's written notification of what changes are to be made. Any other changes made on official records may be made only as the result of a petition approved by the principal and placed on record in the transcript office.

Beyond Letter Grades*

Patrick J. Dowling

AT A TIME when the impulse of secondary education has
been to focus on answering individual student needs and to aid in the
development of the person, the efficacy of using traditional grading
systems to evaluate student growth falls under close critical scrutiny.
Perhaps too much criticism has concentrated on the failure of grading
systems to meet current needs, thus obscuring the active development of
alternative methods of student evaluation; yet, responsible development
has taken place.

One current alternative, functioning since 1970, was developed at
the Glen Oak School in Ohio. Designed to replace the traditional grading
system, recognized as inimical to the school's philosophy of open education, the new system has proved to be a viable, worthwhile alternative
in all respects. Those who are seeking their own answers, which can
be manifold, will find here an account of a fulfilled yet continuously
ongoing search. It is hoped that this text, while not being a dogmatic
manifesto about means and ends, will supply both inspiration· to and
information for all those questioning, or already attempting to alter, the
status quo.

Beginning the Search

Despite continual signs of progress in many areas, sòmething seemed
to be missing at the very heart of the Glen Oak educational process.

* This article is adapted from: Patrick J. Dowling and William Konkoy.
"Beyond Letter Grades." *The Independent School Bulletin* 32(3): 49-51; Febru-
ary 1973. Used with the permission of the National Association of Independent
Schools.

Students, parents, and faculty alike were somewhat uneasy about the evaluation system that had been adopted in lieu of the traditional grade-report scheme. While students confronted trimester barrages of non-uniform, individual course-evaluation reports (raising questions of translation for them and especially for prospective colleges), teachers faced the problem of working in a semi-vacuum, having only ambiguous, departmental guidelines for formulating evaluations to measure and report student cognitive and affective advancement.

Fortunately, the problem was recognized at a time when long-range planning could provide the means to a solution. A proposal for an evaluation workshop was drawn up and submitted to a local foundation that would grant funds for consultants and printing. Faculty members who took part in the workshop were to be paid from the school budget. Originally meant to be a project for the summer of 1971, the workshop eventually began that fall, during faculty-orientation week. One day was set aside specifically for airing opinions of the current evaluation system. This day-long brain-storming session was especially helpful for discussing the inadequacies of the system itself and for articulating the group's apprehensions regarding basic issues: (a) Why "evaluate" rather than "grade"? (b) Who will benefit from evaluations? (c) What are the bases for evaluation? (d) With whom will evaluations communicate? (e) How, specifically, will evaluation be accomplished, and by whom? (f) What are the objectives of evaluation?

These questions could not be answered in an afternoon or a single weekend. Our efforts eventually took two months and included four large-group faculty meetings, several committee and special-group sessions, departmental meetings, consultations with various specialists, and much individual effort.

Continuing the Search

A month-long hiatus in the workshop allowed the faculty to become acclimated to the new school year before meeting again on a Saturday to discuss the evaluation system. With a consultant present to observe the proceedings, the group began by discussing the function of evaluation, and then broke into five subgroups, which reported to the primary group at the close of the day. The result was a number of statements on the function of evaluation.

A special planning committee met during the following week to prepare an outline of the comments made by the various subgroups; the outline was distributed to the faculty along with an agenda for the next meeting. The entire faculty met that Friday to hear from the consultant, who reiterated the necessity of our becoming even more explicit about the function of evaluation and of developing our statements into a set of guidelines that would apply to our situation. Another consultant, a process observer, intervened to keep the group task-oriented and to deal with situations that inhibited the group.

The same five subgroups later met again to discuss the functions of evaluation. Each group was required to define its own statements and to rank them in order of priority. Each of the five then returned to the large group to share their statements and to rank them into even more exact priorities. Failure to achieve this final ranking of all statements resulted in a further task for the planning committee.

The committee met and selected the first-ranking statement from the lists of each of the five subgroups. The overlapping priorities in the resulting master list (*Level I Guidelines for Evaluation* listed below) indicated the consensus of the faculty about the primary purposes which evaluation must accomplish.

Level I Guidelines for Evaluation

• The primary purpose of evaluation is to put us in touch with one another: faculty with faculty, faculty with students, faculty with administration.

• The primary purpose of evaluation is to call the student up to reality and to communicate the above assessment.

• Evaluation is a continuous process of effective communication as needed, when needed, to whomever needs it.

• The primary purpose of evaluation is to report to students their achievement in relation to course objectives.

• In a school whose academic program is both cognitively and affectively oriented, evaluation should provide information about the student's talents, capabilities, and achievements, and should reflect the student's attitudes and interests.

Next, the planning committee worked further to arrange the remaining subgroup statements into ten categories, which were eventually refined by the entire faculty into seven statements as follows:

Level II Guidelines: The Purposes and Functions of Evaluation

• Evaluation should provide students with a wide range of information that includes the affective, cognitive, and psychomotor domains.

Glen Oak School: 1972-1973

Department: _____ Mathematics _____   **Name:** _____

Course: _____ Algebra I _____   **Trimester: I   II   III**

Teacher: _____   **Unit Credit Granted:** _____

Yearly Credit Granted (where applicable): _____

The following areas constitute this trimester's major course content for Algebra I. _____'s mastery of the topics is adequate unless otherwise checked.

Graphing in coordinate plane_____   Interpreting word problems_____

Slope of a line_____   Laws of exponents_____

Determining equation of a line_____   Factoring_____

Multiplying polynomials_____   Solving equations by factoring_____

Solving systems of simultaneous equations_____

She/he demonstrates a working comprehension of _____ percent of the above content.

Improvement In Areas Checked Is Needed. Such improvement would contribute to better understanding and mastery.

Understands what extra help is needed_____   Gives evidence of original thought_____

Utilizes opportunities for extra help_____   Strives for deeper understanding_____

Completes prescribed preparation on time_____   Responds favorably to suggestion_____

Completes written work in good form_____   Takes a positive approach_____

Initiates questions when material is not clear_____   Respects the rights, opinions, abilities of others_____

Thinks before asking questions_____   Manifests a sense of responsibility for the group's progress_____

Is present and ready to begin class on time_____

*Comments:*_____

_____

_____

Glen Oak School: 1972-1973

Department: _____English_____ **Name:**_____

Course: _____American Literature_____ **Trimester: I II III**

Teacher:_____ **Unit Credit Granted:** _____

**Yearly Credit Granted
(where applicable):** _____

The American Literature section of American Studies is designed to corre-late literature with the historical periods and spirits of American man. The second trimester has dealt with: (a) overall view of spirits of American Literature; (b) the Revolutionary Spirit with a study of *A Separate Peace* and individually chosen war themes; (c) regionalism and local color short stories; (d) the Westward Movement—with special study of Mark Twain and *Adventures of Huck Finn;* and (e) Roaring 20's and *The Great Gatsby.*

Emphasis is placed on appreciation, analysis, and interpretation of major works and is designed to develop and strengthen the skills of reading for appreciation and for understanding, discussion, and writing.

Content—The student:

Comprehends the literal and figurative meaning of the works studied_____

Transfers knowledge and appreciation from history to literature_____

Grapples with material and makes it her/his own_____

Draws conclusions and forms own opinions_____

Skills—The student:

Participates effectively in group discussion_____

Listens attentively to others_____

Asks provocative questions in group discussion_____

Has ability to organize and develop an essay_____

Has and employs an ability to use the proper mechanics of writing_____

Uses outside reference tools to supplement study_____

Has ability to determine thesis statement and to write sentence outline_____

Attitudes—The student:

Is open to the variety of literary experiences_____

Shows an openness to and respect for the opinions of others_____

Allows herself/himself an open response to the material_____

Comes prepared to take an active role in classwork_____

*Comments:*_____
_____

• Evaluation should help students and teachers to develop skill in: (a) self-appraisal, and (b) self-understanding and self-acceptance.

• The evaluation process should assist the teacher in developing insights about the student.

• Evaluation should be an ongoing process that points the way to and stimulates further growth.

• Evaluation should serve as a motivating force.

• A written record of the evaluation should be available to parents, academic institutions, and other agencies.

• Evaluation should provide a basis for program planning and design.

That consensus was reached on such a basic issue as the function of evaluation was indicative of the group's solidarity. Belief in the validity of this consensus was reinforced by the similarity of our findings to those of the Association for Supervision and Curriculum Development, which has stated that:

. . . to do its fundamental task, evaluation must perform five tasks. It must:
• Facilitate self-evaluation;
• Encompass all the objectives;
• Facilitate teaching and learning;
• Generate records appropriate to various uses;
• Facilitate decision-making on curriculum and educational policy.[2]

Such support was indeed heartening; of even greater value, however, was the growth the group experienced by being involved in the process itself. The statements we formulated gave us an understanding of what we were about in a way that no preconceived, predigested, preselected system ever could.

The work that followed involved itemization of departmental objectives and goals as they related to student development and learning. These objectives were then reported to the large group and later tested against the guidelines to check their validity in terms of evaluation. Completed departmental objectives, in the following weeks, were refined and checked again according to the system we had adopted.

Our final step was to arrange a format for reporting, which involved record keeping and transcripts—a difficult task for the guidance counselor of college-bound students. Such counselors, in this system, must collect

[2] Fred T. Wilhelms, editor. *Evaluation as Feedback and Guide.* Washington, D.C.: Association for Supervision and Curriculum Development, 1967.

all individual course evaluations for a given student, abstract each evaluation, and complete a composite of these abstracts to be sent out as a formal transcript. Other pertinent data, such as standardized test scores, are included in each transcript and sent to college admissions officers with a covering letter of explanation.

As of this writing, all of the college admissions officers to whom we have sent these transcripts have accepted our format of evaluation and reporting, many of them enthusiastically. One director of admissions indicated that his "first reaction was to . . . warn of the impending dangers with regard to trifling with the traditional educational system. However, after reflecting on the subject and taking into account the frustrations of some high school students with the traditional system, my reaction is 'more power to you.'"

Support for the new evaluation method was quickly communicated to students, parents, and the school's board of trustees, thus mollifying their fears and greatly bolstering their confidence in the system we had adopted. For the faculty, this support justified the months of effort spent up to that point.

The workshop ended in time for us to use its results for evaluation during the first trimester, following which we found some further tests and refinements needed. Certain areas of individual evaluation needed reworking for various reasons, and certain evaluations proved unwieldy, needing revision for purposes of record keeping.

The second trimester saw a number of changes in individual evaluation, with still more refinements to follow. Another consultant visited the school for three days in February 1972, to present the faculty and administration with valuable information gained from having discussed the newly revised evaluation system with students, parents, and teachers. Feedback has been and will continue to be an important part of the ongoing refinement of our evaluation procedures.

The Ongoing Search

Since evaluation of student learning is only one small part of the instructional system, it became necessary, in the fall of 1972, to supplement the progress made in the evaluation workshop with still more professional input. Frances Link, international implementer for *Man: A Course of Study*, led the Glen Oak faculty through a three-day session, using the content of *Man*, a model of curriculum design, to focus on teaching strategies and learning styles. The impetus of the session confirmed the notion that repertoires of teaching behavior must be expanded in order √ to accommodate and facilitate the many learning styles of students, and that such an expansion could be aided by the use of many evaluation strategies which lead us to learn much about student learning processes. The idea of evaluation, then, becomes even more expanded when considered essentially as a means, not an end, in the effort to achieve more effective learning.

The redefinition of evaluation has had great effect on the day-to-day classroom situation. Inasmuch as we learned the importance of analyzing course objectives through the evaluation workshop, our entire approach to course structuring has now been geared to fulfilling valid objectives. We are forced, as a result of Frances Link's workshop, to reassess objectives on specific levels, such as our daily involvement with students and with course content. The faculty now perceives objectives as necessarily fluid, coinciding with and fulfilling—yet not stifled by—the broader objectives underlying the scope of course planning. We are now aware that we must ask of each day and each student contact, "Why am I doing what I am doing, when I am doing it?" Only in this way can a sound basis be established on which evaluation can fulfill all its varied purposes.

—Part IV—

Changing the System

THOSE FAMILIAR WITH values clarification understand that our beliefs and attitudes are not values unless we act upon or do what we say in a consistent manner. Many have affirmed support for grading reform; few have instituted changes in grading practice. This section includes not only a practical guide for implementing grading reform, but also actual accounts of how individuals have struggled to implement reforms, and suggestions of how certain pitfalls can be avoided. The results, as each reformer attests, come only with time, pain, and sometimes laughter. The myths die slowly, but they do die.

Dear Parents: What You Want To Know Isn't Necessarily What We Want To Tell You!

Lois Borland Hart

THINK BACK TO the last time that you as an educator were responsible for sending to a student's home any sort of evaluation or report card. Picture one of your own students and reflect upon the different sorts of information that you wanted to pass on to the child's parents. What was the essence of what you wished to convey? Perhaps it was your joy upon seeing an improvement in mathematics skills, perhaps it was a concern about the student's problems with other children in the class.

What were the means that the evaluation form (be it report card or progress report) allotted to you in your efforts to convey what you felt was essential to those parents?

Did you ever wonder just what kinds of information the parents, for their part, want to get from the forms that teachers write and schools send out?

Try to think back to the last time that you (if you are a parent) received a report of some kind about one of your children. What did you really want to find out about? Perhaps it was how your child's work compared to that of other children similar in age and intelligence. Maybe you wanted to know whether there was any way you could help your child to adjust to a recent geographical relocation. In what ways did the report card or progress report sent to you from your child's school convey the critical information you needed? Or, did it fail to do so?

Throughout the history of schooling, innumerable varieties of reports have been sent to parents by schools: letter grades, percentages, pass/fail notations, checklists, rating scales, behavioral descriptions, and narratives. As I reviewed the various reporting systems available to me as an educator, I began to ask myself, "Which system will provide me with the opportunity to record the kinds of information about my students that I want to send to their homes?"

I realized that several of the options available to me were limited in their ability to say what I wanted to parents. But then, I also realized that we, as educators, had never taken the time to really find out what parents want to know about their children's progress. I asked myself, "What *do* parents want to know and will it be the same kinds of information that I as an educator have been sending?"

It seemed to me, therefore, that before we educators make a final decision as to which reporting method to use in suchool, we first need to find out the answers to the following questions:

• What information do educators feel is the most and the least important to give parents concerning their child's progress?

• In what areas do parents most and least desire information from their child's school?

• In what ways are the kinds of information the parents desire to receive similar or dissimilar to that which the educators desire to send?

Four assumptions underlie this research. First, because reports from the school to the home have been the primary means of communication in the past, use of a reporting system of some kind will continue. Second, the dissatisfaction expressed by many educators and parents with currently used reporting systems may be partly caused by the fact that present methods do not fully meet the needs of educators who value one kind of information and the needs of parents who prefer something different. The third assumption is that effective communication between the school and the home must be two-way communication. From what I have seen and read about the process of making a change in a reporting system, rarely does the school try to determine what parents want to know about their child's progress *before* a decision concerning the reporting method is made. The fourth assumption is that improved communication can benefit the school, the parents, and the children. The process suggested here can increase understanding between educators charged with a child's education and the parents of that child.

How can we find out what the school wants to send and the parents want to receive? Responses to the following questionnaire help to answer this question. (Methods used to develop, utilize, and evaluate this questionnaire are discussed later in this chapter.)

PART I

Directions: Think about a particular group of students or a particular child as you complete this questionnaire. Rank the items in each category according to how important it is for you to have information sent to the child's/children's home(s). Place a number 1 next to the item that is the most important to send, a number 2 next to the second most important item, and so forth.

Information on the Academic Progress of the Child

_____What is the child's capacity for learning and how does his/her work compare with his/her ability?

_____What specifically is the child learning in school?

_____In what ways has the child's work improved or slipped since the last report?

_____How does the child's achievement compare to that of the national average for children of this age group?

_____How does the child's work compare to the work of other children in the class?

Information on How the Child Learns at School

_____Does the child know how to use wisely the time not preplanned by the teacher?

_____Does the child learn better in large groups, in small groups, or in independent learning situations?

_____Does the child apply what he/she has learned to situations beyond the immediate lesson?

_____What materials does the child use in his/her learning activities?

Information on How the Home Can Help the Student Do Better in School

_____How can the parent help the child with the problems that result from physical and emotional growth?

_____Are there physical and/or emotional problems that are interfering with the child's learning and resulting in his/her need for professional help?

_____How can the parent help the child establish better social relationships with other children?

_____Are there ways the parents can help their child do better in his/her schoolwork?

Information on How the Child Conforms to School Standards

_____Does the child pay attention in class and does he/she follow directions?

_____Does the child begin his/her work promptly and complete it on time?

_____Is the child's appearance acceptable according to school standards?

_____Does the child keep his/her personal materials and property in order?

Information on the Child's Social Adjustment
with His/Her Classmates

_____Does the child ever offer to help others?

_____Does the child respect the rights and property of others?

_____What is the attitude of the other children toward this child?

_____Does the child work and play well with others in group situations?

Information on the School's Goals and Operation

_____What are the long- and short-term goals of the school?

_____What is the school doing to accomplish these goals?

_____How is the school's faculty selected and organized?

_____In what ways is the child evaluated and how often does this happen?

PART II

Directions: The following is a summary listing the six categories of information. Rank each category according to how important it is to you as an educator in sending home information from the school. Place a number 1 next to the category that is most important; place a number 2 next to the second most important category, and so forth.

_____Information on the academic progress of the child.

_____Information on how the child learns at school.

_____Information on how the home can help the student to do better in school.

_____Information on how the child conforms to school standards.

_____Information on the child's social adjustment with his/her classmates.

_____Information on the school's goals and organization.

By now you are familiar with six categories of information that schools often send to parents and some very specific kinds of information within each category. In 1972, I administered this questionnaire to a group of teachers and parents of elementary students in the Westhill School District, a suburban school system near Syracuse, New York. The school district served approximately 15,000 people who were in a predominately white, middle and upper-middle socioeconomic group.

Some of these same teachers had been a part of a report card study committee charged with the task of reviewing alternatives to the traditional grading currently being used in the district. The administration of the school district agreed to have my master's thesis research project implemented in the district (where I was a teacher at the time) because the research was seen as providing helpful information to the district as it moved toward a change in its method of reporting to parents.

The categories of information selected for the questionnaire were determined after careful study of current literature on the topic, actual report cards, and parent-conference forms. The words were carefully analyzed to avoid ambiguity. Eventually the list was narrowed down to a more manageable one of six categories. The order of each category in the questionnaire was determined by giving each a number, then drawing lots.

The school district was involved in a one-year pilot project on report cards using a written narrative report in combination with parent-teacher conferences. This new form was used with a sample of students in kindergarten, and in grades one, three, and five. The 208 sets of parents whose children were in the pilot project made up the sample for this research. All sixty elementary teachers were asked to participate.

An aim of the original research was to find out if the parents of high-achieving children desire information different from that of the parents of lower-achieving children. Furthermore, the questionnaire requested information on the parents (age, sex, education) and inquired as to the number of children in the family. Teachers provided information on their age, sex, education, amount and kinds of teaching experience, and their range of experience with various reporting methods. The research was an attempt to see whether any of these variables made a difference in what parents desired to receive and teachers wanted to send.

Parents received the questionnaires by mail, while teachers obtained them at their respective schools. All responses were anonymous.

What kinds of information did parents desire most and desire least to receive from the school about their child? What kinds of information did teachers want to send to these parents? The following is a summary of the research findings.

Given six general categories of information, parents ranked first their desire for information about their child's academic progress which the teachers ranked third. (See Table 1.) Parents ranked "How the child learns" second, while this category was ranked first by the teachers. Least important to the parents was information on the "School's goals and organization," an area ranked fifth by the teachers. Teachers ranked "How the child conforms to school standards" as least important, while parents ranked this category fourth.

What was most important to teachers and parents within each category? Table 2. shows this information.

It was found that factors such as the parents' sex, level of education, and the achievement level of their child did not significantly affect the parents' desire for a particular kind of information from the school.

Categories of Information	All Parents	All Teachers
Academic progress	1	3
How the child learns	2	1
How the home can help	3	4
How the child conforms to school standards	4	6
Child's social adjustment with classmates	5	2
School's goals and organization	6	5

Table 1. Rankings of Categories of Information
by Parents and Teachers

General Category	Specific Information Most Desired by Parents	Specific Information Most Desired by Teachers
Academic progress	What is my child's capacity and how does his/her work compare with his/her ability?	Same
How the child learns	Does my child apply what he/she has learned to situations beyond the immediate lesson?	Same
How the home can help	How can I help my child with the problems that result from physical and emotional growth?	Same
How the child conforms to school standards	Does my child pay attention in class and does he/she follow directions?	Same
School's goals and organization	In what way is my child evaluated and how often does this happen?	What are the long- and short-term goals of the school?

Table 2. Rankings of Specific Information
Within Six Categories

Factors such as the teacher's age, education, and teaching experience did not significantly affect the kinds of information that teachers desired to convey to parents.

Although the findings of this research may be interesting, their value was primarily to the school district in which the research was done. It would be dangerous to generalize beyond this sample about the information priorities of all parents and the reporting preferences of all teachers.

The realistic application of this research to other schools would involve, not generalization, but an adaptation of the *process* used. Individual schools and/or school districts can replicate the process outlined here in order to find out for themselves exactly what they want to tell parents and how that relates to the information that parents desire. In this way, educators can make their final decision an informed one based on essential information.

Further information can be obtained by extending the groups sampled to include administrators and school board members and then comparing the results of all of the questionnaires.

Another method I have used successfully researches the problem more informally. It begins with a cross section of parents and educators gathered together, perhaps at a Parent-Teacher Association meeting. Since some of the educators will also be parents of school-age children, they may want to "think as a parent" rather than as an educator when responding to questions.

First, parents are asked to think about a particular child and his or her unique needs. Then the educators are asked to think about a particular group of children or even one child. With particular individuals in mind, everyone is asked to privately fill out one of the questionnaires. While the group does this, six large signs, each indicating one of the categories of information used in my formal survey, are taped to different places in the room.

When everyone is finished, each parent is asked to stand by the sign listing the information that he or she feels is most important. After the parents have gathered beneath the signs, they are asked to explain briefly their reasons for selecting a particular category.

An extremely important ground rule is that each speaker has the right to be heard without being challenged by others. The purpose of this activity is to share viewpoints and not to argue the merits of one's viewpoint. If participants do argue with one another, others may be reticent to give their views. To encourage the expression of all viewpoints is one purpose of the experiment.

After a sample from each group of parents has been heard, the parents are asked to sit down. Now each educator is asked to stand by the category which he or she feels reflects the most valuable information. Again, verbal explanations are encouraged. The floor may then be opened to questions that clarify a point, but do not challenge what was said earlier.

The entire process may then be repeated to ascertain those categories which are of secondary importance to parents and educators. I have found that the parents' group and the educators' group usually tend to select the same two categories within their top three rankings. Thus, it is helpful to have the two groups realize, through such a visible demonstration of their choices, how close their values really are.

Participants are usually very much interested in how each group ranks the specific items within a major category. A vote of hands will give a quick reading of where sentiment on these values lies.

Depending on the energy level and the interest of the group, all six rankings can be explored in detail, but it is more likely that the participants will tire after about three categories are explored fully. I would therefore suggest that the top two and the last rankings be the three to be explored. This process will stimulate a good deal of thought and small groups made up of parents and educators may have follow-up discussions as a conclusion to the evening.

Adapting the Process

If you are thinking of using the general process described here, I would like to make two more suggestions: First, consider changing the categories (the major or specific items) to fit the community and educational setting in which you work. For instance, educators who have used this questionnaire have been trying to modify the category, "How the child conforms to school standards," because of the connotation of the word "conform." Others have noted that there are no items that deal with information about a child's self-knowledge. You may also decide that a certain phrase needs rewording to clarify the meaning for your community.

Second, use this process as the first step in your attempt to make a change in reporting procedures. Leave enough time for participants to think through all of the issues raised. Follow up with a review of alternatives available, along with a list of pros and cons for each alternative. At this point, the question that should be continually asked is, "How would these alternatives provide us, as educators, with the opportunity to send parents the kinds of information that we want to send?" Also ask yourself, "How would this alternative provide us, as parents, with the kinds of information that we want about our child?"

The process described here, which was based on a formal research technique and later adapted to a more informal means of gathering data, should provide educators with the answers to key questions in their quest to modify reporting procedures. The answers to these questions, by leading to the selection of appropriate progress reports or report cards, should increase the satisfaction of both educators and parents with the new system.

The MAP Cycle:
A Change Process for Grading Reform

James A. Bellanca

WHEN A FAMILY plans its summer vacation, a salesman anticipates a trip, or a truck driver receives a cross-state assignment, a highway map is pulled from the glove compartment and spread out on a table. The map indicates alternate routes, scenic vistas, ongoing road repair, and distances between towns. It records historic sites, population density, and rest stops; it distinguishes major and minor roads, big cities, and small towns; it suggests direction, distance, and location.

As years pass, a map changes character. At one time in long past years, uncharted territory waited for the first pioneer to step into the virgin forest. The first pioneers, guided by instinct and nature's trails, hacked paths through unmapped regions. Map makers, following rough charts and slim trails, recorded the peculiarities of terrain. As new families followed, towns grew, farms were plotted, and details were entered on the surveyor's map. The modern map, intricate in its abundance of detail, is collected, studied, marked, and remarked as it guides the traveler.

The creation, use, and evaluation of a map simulates the process of change in a variety of ways:

The change process is dynamic. A perfect map does not exist. On the day a map rolls from the printer's press, it is outdated. The map maker must restudy the terrain and refine his product. The process of creating a map never ceases.

The change process individuates according to need. A map maker designs each map for a different purpose: travel, engineering, demography, geography. He creates a product which each user may adapt: the family camping, the salesman traveling, the tourist sightseeing.

The change process distinguishes creativity, use, and evaluation as growth components. It recognizes that individuals have varying competence to utilize each component and encourages each individual to give priority to competency development through self-direction. The map maker, the bridge builder, the geologist, and the gas station attendant may use the same map with different degrees of social value or personal satisfaction. The geologist locates a shallow river bed; the bridge builder uses the discovery to plan a new highway; the map maker records the new bridge; the gas station attendant points out the distance saved by the new construction. The traveling tourist need not judge the contribution of the previous mappers; he or she is thankful for the time saved by the map.

The change process values goals not as final objectives which terminate a process, but as clarifying elements in a self-regenerating cycle. A road map shows few roads with a definite start and end. Side roads flow into secondary highways which feed into major expressways; expressways dissolve into turnpikes which feed back into the secondary routes. A father who plans to travel to Ann Arbor, Michigan, may trace his path visually from his home on Chicago's Devon Avenue out to Edens expressway, south to the Calumet extension which blends into the east-bound Indiana Turnpike. At Gary West, the interchange cloverleafs into I-94 which travels north and east to Ann Arbor exits and beyond. To close the cycle, he reverses his direction and his eyes carry him over the same route or a variety of alternates back to his home.

Using Educational Maps

The MAP cycle processes development through these stages: measuring, actualizing, and performing:

M: In the *measuring stage,* the change agent identifies: (a) purpose of change, (b) available resources, (c) obstacles to change, and (d) alternative paths to cyclical completion.

A: In the *actualizing stage,* the change agent selects: (a) goals, (b) strategies, and (c) evaluation method.

P: In the *performing stage,* the change agent: (a) guides implementation and (b) evaluates the process and products of MAP.

I. Measuring

    A. Identifying purpose of change

        1. Why do we want this change?
            a. What weaknesses do we hope to eliminate from the present system?
            b. What innovations do we want? What responses do we want from teachers, from students, from others, as a result of the changes? To what extent do we wish attitudinal and/or behavioral changes?
            c. What negative side-effects do we want to avoid for the system, for teachers, for students, for others? To what extent do we wish to avoid negative changes in attitude and/or in behavior?

        2. What are our priorities for change?
            a. What positive and negative consequences are likely to result from these changes?
            b. What are our priorities after we have considered consequences?

    B. Identifying suitable resources

        1. Given the priorities, what resources are needed?
            a. Which faculty, administrators, students, parents, community representatives (identify boundaries from which community resources can reasonably be drawn) can contribute expertise?
            b. What media resources (TV, school library, public libraries, personal libraries, film, videotapes, cassette recordings, simulation games, workshops, seminars, university classes, night school courses) can provide the information?

        2. What funds are available to finance expertise in and an information search for areas in which voluntary expertise or information access is *not* possible locally?
            a. Travel expense funds for consultant time?
            b. Travel expense and stipend payment funds for consultant time?
            c. Media purchase (books, videotapes, film rental)?
            d. Travel expense funds for staff visits to consultants or staff participation in workshops, institutes, conferences?

        3. How can the available local expertise, information, or available funds best serve our purposes? (Rank order.)

        4. How can we best organize our resources to accomplish our priorities?

        5. Who will assume which responsibilities?
            a. Who will seek and organize expertise?
            b. Who will seek and organize information?
            c. Who will research media possibilities?
            d. Who will determine availability and use of funds?

        6. How will the committee process this information?

    C. Identifying Obstacles

        1. Which persons (students, parents, teachers, administrators?) will oppose the change priorities?
            a. What form will the opposition take?
            b. To what extent will they oppose the change?

MAP—The Process of Change

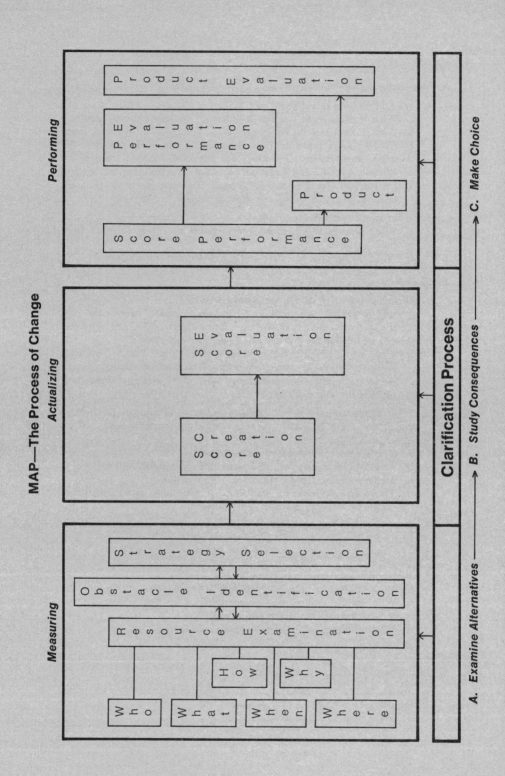

Measuring

Who
What
When
Where
How
Why

Resource Examination

Obstacle Identification

Strategy Selection

Actualizing

SC
Score
creation

SE
Score
evaluation

Performing

Score Performance

PE
Performance
evaluation

Product

PP
Product Evaluation

Clarification Process

A. Examine Alternatives ⟶ B. Study Consequences ⟶ C. Make Choice

    2. What reasoning will substantiate these oppositional responses?

    3. How can we deal with this opposition in a fair manner?

  D. Identifying Alternate Paths

    1. Which paths appear most likely to accomplish our intent?
      a. To what extent will each help or hinder?
      b. What are the consequences attendant on each route?

    2. What identifying obstacle is the top priority among the alternates?

II. Actualizing

  A. Detailing the MAP

    1. Considering the priority path selected, how can we clearly state the goals we wish to accomplish?
      a. What changes in behavior and attitude do we wish to have occur?
      b. What modifications of structure, content, or process are required?

    2. Which strategies will we employ to accomplish our goals?
      a. What alternatives are available?
      b. What are the consequences of each alternative?
      c. What are our priorities based on our value system?
      d. Who has what responsibilities for implementing strategies?
      e. What are the parameters controlling implementation?

    3. By what means will we evaluate the extent to which we accomplish our goals?
      a. What anticipated or unanticipated changes will we value highly?
      b. What are the criteria for success?

  B. Evaluating the MAP

    1. Considering desired change and possible change, does MAP indicate a probable degree of success?

    2. To what extent are the goals and strategies consistent with our values?

    3. To what extent are the goals and strategies consistent with each other?

    4. To what extent are modifications needed for MAP integrity?

    5. To what extent are other possible changes needed in MAP?

    6. To what extent are responsibilities equally and fairly distributed according to ability, interest, and concern?

    7. To what extent have we considered the full consequences of this change for each constituent?

III. Performing

  A. Implementing Strategies

    1. To what extent are we remaining flexible by adapting strategies to meet unexpected contingencies?
      a. How responsive are we to individual need?
      b. How sensitive are we to feelings uncovered by stress associated with change?

   c. How imaginative are we in coping with unexpected problems?

2. To what extent are we remaining consistent with our values?
   a. To what extent are we justifying strategy on the basis of objectives?
   b. To what extent are we rationalizing erroneous assumptions?

3. To what extent is each individual maintaining his or her responsibility?

B. Evaluating MAP

   1. What positive changes, planned through MAP, resulted from this process?
      a. What new understandings, attitudes, values, behaviors, skills, processes, products, performances, or competencies were developed consistent with MAP objectives?
      b. What positive changes, not planned through MAP, resulted?

   2. What negative changes occurred?
      a. Why are these changes viewed negatively?
      b. What was the cause of each?
      c. How can we rectify each?

   3. What changes, planned through MAP, did not occur?
      a. Why didn't these changes occur?
      b. Does a need exist now, for these changes?
      c. If so, how can we facilitate these changes?

   4. Given the results of MAP, which changes, not previously planned through MAP, should receive priority attention in a new MAP?
      a. Why are these changes needed?
      b. Who will assume responsibility to redirect MAP to process the newly identified needs?

The Change Agent in Grading Reform

Howard Kirschenbaum

Changing a school's grading and evaluation system is one of the most difficult innovations to introduce in public or private education. New approaches in one's own classroom usually can be effected much more simply, but try to get one's colleagues to change and see the resistance emerge. Few issues are liable to stir stronger emotions or generate greater controversy.

The reason is simple. Grading and evaluation practices are integrally related to almost every other aspect of a school's functioning—how power is distributed and used, faculty-student relations, educational priorities, instructional procedures, administrative politics, parental aspirations, the job market, and the like. One does not simply describe three startling research studies and give several arguments supporting new grading alternatives to a school faculty and expect everyone to join the reform bandwagon. It is a much more profound reform that the grading/evaluation innovator is suggesting, whether he or she realizes it or not.

To be a change agent in grading reform requires the perspective of an organizational development specialist. A careful strategy is needed. Such a strategy must be created anew in each school and system, depending on the realities of that organization. Some issues, however, are common to all educational systems. Following are 12 questions which must be faced at some point by the change agent in grading reform.

1. *What are our long-range educational goals?* Most educators are more interested in the learning process than the grading-evaluation process. But they have learned that evaluation can be an integral part of

the learning process and that a school's evaluation system often influences the type of learning that takes place. Grading reform, then, is usually a means to an end—a strategy designed to make a certain type of learning possible. In this context the most basic question the reformers must answer is: What type of education do I value? What kind of learning process do I want to see in our school or system?

2. *What kind of evaluation-reporting system is most consistent with the kind of learning I most value?* Clarity on the previous question makes an answer to the second question possible. It also raises other questions. Are there several evaluation systems that are consistent with my view of education? Are there other legitimate views of education and, therefore, other evaluation systems which should be legitimized? Is my ideal a school with one learning-evaluation system for everyone, or should there be two or more options? Finally, what kind of evaluation system (and simultaneously, what kind of teacher-learning system) shall we work toward?

3. *What are our alternatives for planning and implementing the change?* People have tried myriad methods—committees, petitions, going through channels, going outside of channels, position papers, referenda, articles in the school newspaper, a copy of *Wad-Ja-Get?* [1] in each teacher's box, and so on. For every expert who tells us to start at the top and get the key administrators on our side, there are just as many who say start at the bottom so the faculty and students do not feel something is being imposed upon them. What other alternatives are there? What is a wise strategy? The answers will vary in different situations. By selecting a strategy from alternatives, however, with full consideration given to the probable consequences of the different alternatives, the change agent's choices are more likely to be effective. The next several issues are more specific subheadings of this question.

4. *What resources do we have available, within the system and without, to facilitate the change process?* Who will support the change? Who will provide expertise in the various areas of need? What information will provide the needed insight and direction? What funds are available? With all the resources carefully identified and each applied to the situation at hand, the possibility of success increases.

5. *What obstacles are we likely to face? How might we deal with these?* Rather than being defeated by unexpected resistance and compli-

[1] Howard Kirschenbaum, Sidney B. Simon, and Rodney W. Napier. *Wad-Ja-Get? The Grading Game in American Education.* New York: Hart Publishing Company, Inc., 1971.

cations, it makes more sense to identify the obstacles ahead of time. In that way, steps can be taken to eliminate, minimize, or deal with an anticipated obstacle when it occurs. To pretend that everything will unfold smoothly is unrealistic and self-defeating.

6. *How can we build a supportive climate?* It is in an atmosphere of trust and openness that people are most willing to change. When they feel attacked or threatened, they cling most firmly to the old, secure ways. So the change agent asks: How can we eliminate or minimize student-faculty discord? How can we keep lines of communication open? How can we prevent polarization—"us *versus* them"? How can we counter student *versus* student competition and parental worry over college admissions? Even, as a last resort, if some confrontation is built into the change strategy, the change agent knows that after the confrontation, people will have to begin communicating with each other again. Ultimately, the plan needs almost everyone's support to succeed, and that can only come about in a supportive climate.

7. *Have we involved all interested groups in the planning and implementation process?* Sooner or later, a group that is left out of the change process subtly or dramatically can begin to undermine the new system. Students, faculty, administrators, parents, community members, school board, all have some stake in the issue—especially an issue as controversial as grading. Not everyone must be involved from the very beginning, although that is one alternative; and there is no one right way to involve them (for example, community control, parent advisory board, student control). But unless all those affected feel included, unless they feel supportive of the change, innovation will have that much less of a chance for success. Many a grading reform has died because of the backlash generated by an excluded segment of the school community.

8. *Have we identified the* leadership *in the various subgroups and made plans for enlisting their support?* It is often more economical to put one's efforts into winning over a key figure in the faculty or student body, for example, than to spend an equal amount of time and energy trying to relate to *every* teacher or student. It is key administrators, department chairpersons, student representatives, sports or even gang leaders, teacher association representatives, PTA officers, and the like, who can reach more of their constituents than the change agent could ever hope to influence directly.

9. *What means other than lecturing can we use to let people know what we are doing and to involve them in our efforts?* By talking *at* someone, you reinforce the idea that it is your plan which you want to see

implemented. By talking *with* them, they can feel that it is also their plan. Large group presentations are often necessary. But only in smaller groups, where people can talk through their own concerns and have their questions answered, will they come to feel a commitment to the change. When shall these groups meet? Who shall lead them? What shall the format and the expected outcomes be? What will follow these meetings? There are many possibilities. It is at this grass roots level, though, that the fate of an innovation is often decided.

10. *What other changes will a change in our grading-evaluation lead to? How can we best prepare ourselves for these secondary changes?* Grading reform is not a panacea. A new evaluation approach makes possible new ways of learning and new ways of relating; it does not automatically bring about the joyful utopia that the romantic reformers promise. Therefore, how can we develop new curricula, new resources, and new school structures appropriate to our new evaluation system? (Better yet, vice versa: What kind of learning do we value? Then, how can we evaluate it?) Who will take on what responsibilities to see that our reforms go deeper than the superficial reporting symbols on the transcript?

11. *How shall we evaluate the new system?* As with any new program that has existed for a time, some people will want to maintain it and some will want to return to the previous system. Innovators who believe their new approach has merit, would probably do well to muster objective evidence that their plan is working. Otherwise, some negative incident, some change in administration, or some random event might be enough to start the whole debate over again, with the tide turned in the opposite direction. Solid evidence of success can stem the tide of temporary reaction and allow the innovation the time it deserves to prove itself.

12. *After implementation, then what?* Having a new system accepted and implemented is only part of the change agent's job. Like a newly planted tree, reform needs to be properly nurtured and protected. How can we help all the parties learn to use the new system effectively and to keep improving it? Who will have what responsibilities once the system is adopted? How can we evaluate our efforts? What further changes will be needed? When questions like these are not faced early, a change that got off to a good start can soon begin to falter and eventually fail.

To summarize, it is a very different thing to try to bring grading reform to an entire school or system than it is to change evaluation practices in one's own classroom. In any complex organization, there are numerous variables and pitfalls that must be planned for if the change is to be effected successfully. I have attempted to raise some of the major questions I think proponents of evaluation reform need to deal with seriously. I have not tried to answer these questions, because I have neither the time nor the wisdom to formulate a plan of change for the hundreds of different situations in which grading alternatives are being considered. Hopefully, these questions will spur the individuals in each situation to think more carefully about the issues involved in change and, therefore, to make decisions which are, in the final analysis, more rewarding.

The Day the Consultant
Looked at Our Grading System[*]

*Sidney B. Simon, Howard Kirschenbaum,
and Rodney W. Napier*

A CONTROVERSY OVER the grading system has been raging among students and faculty at West High, a large suburban high school outside of one of America's largest cities.

It all began with an argument in one English class on the question, "Can you 'grade' poetry?" The argument spread and drew more and more teachers and students into rapidly polarizing camps.

Some of the students put out a position paper on the grading problem. It was circulated throughout the school. One class made a commitment to change the school's grading system, come hell or high water. A very successful alumnus came back to West High to address an assembly. He had won every academic honor in the book, but he caught everyone off guard with a speech consisting of reasons why he now felt that his formal education was a pointless charade because he had succumbed to the pressure to get grades.

He stirred up a lot of discussion. Students became enthusiastic and concerned. The faculty grew nervous, and the administration knew it was sitting on a powder keg. Rumors flew. Anxious parents called the school

* The above article is reprinted with permission from: *Phi Delta Kappan* 51: 476-79; May 1970. It also appears in: Howard Kirschenbaum, Sidney B. Simon, and Rodney W. Napier. *Wad-Ja-Get? The Grading Game in American Education.* New York: Hart Publishing Company, Inc., 1971. Copyright 1971 by Hart Publishing Company, Inc.

to warn Mr. Fusari, the principal, not to do anything to jeopardize their sons' and daughters' chances of getting into good colleges. Some faculty members quietly encouraged students to bring about the revolution in marks.

Just before the action reported . . . a group of moderate and concerned teachers approached Mr. Fusari, telling him that he must take action. They argued that grading practice was already a major issue for the students and that the faculty had better come to terms with the movement pretty quickly. They asked for a special faculty meeting to discuss the grading problem.

Mr. Fusari agreed to call such a meeting. His style was to bring in an old and trusted friend, Mr. Blanc, from the local state teachers college, who would give a solid, unexceptional talk to the faculty on what the research says, etc.—nothing controversial, fair to all sides. In his cliché-driven career, Mr. Fusari is firmly committed to the notion that "more light and less heat" is needed these days. But the special faculty meeting must be held this coming Friday if it's to be held at all.

As fate would have it, Mr. Fusari's education prof can't make it, but he finds a substitute, a younger member of the department. Mr. Blanc doesn't know much about the new fellow's views on grades, but he does know that the neophyte has a solid research background and "should do a very competent and professional job for you, Mr. Fusari."

The substitute is invited and he accepts. The meeting is announced the next day to the faculty. What follows is an account of the meeting.

The sun splashed through big windows and painted the library with pale yellow streaks. It was Friday, and Mr. Ingles looked down at the students filling the walkways and the grounds below.

"Lucky stiffs," Mr. Ingles muttered to no one in particular, as he turned from the window and headed for the tarnished metal coffee urn on the long center table.

"What's the matter, Mr. Ingles?" Miss Doyle said, "Don't you like donuts?"

"Not at 3:15 on a Friday afternoon," he told her, filling his clinical-white styrofoam cup with black coffee, "but since you insist." He fingered what he thought was a jelly-filled donut and bit into it.

"I don't insist," the lady answered, "but they were made by my fourth-period class especially for the faculty, and so I'll insist for *them*."

Jelly spurted from the opposite end of the donut and dripped onto Mr. Ingles' hand. "Well, give them my compliments," he said, as he walked to a seat, licking the jelly from his fingers, "and an 'A' for effort."

"Thanks," she smiled back at him, and then turned to watch a stranger come into the room, flanked on both sides by Mr. Fusari and Mr. Crewson.

Mr. Ingles sat down, away from the other teachers, and sipped on his coffee, waiting for the meeting to get under way. He didn't like these faculty meetings, especially the ones that were called without notice, and even more especially when it was Friday. He had far more important things to do than listen to some college professor talk about grades.

"This is Dr. Richard Miller from Central State. He's in the Psychology Department there," Mr. Crewson was saying to Miss Doyle. "He's going to be talking to us this afternoon."

"Hi," Miss Doyle greeted the young-looking, slightly built man. "We have coffee and donuts. What can I get you?"

"I'd really like something," Dr. Miller said politely, "but I think I'd better go to work." He pointed to some equipment being wheeled in by two boys from the A-V Department. "So we can all get out of here at a reasonable hour." He smiled and nodded and then walked toward the boys. On the cart was an overhead projector. He directed the boys to set it up, then turned his attention to a small, strange-looking gadget that resembled a miniature version of a computer, somewhat similar to those one might see on television during election-night coverage.

Though a substitute for another speaker Mr. Fusari had originally invited, Dr. Miller felt assured. He was excited and as he worked he went over what he was planning to say to the West High faculty—or to any faculty he would ever get the chance to talk to on the subject of grades. He watched the teachers filing in. He heard one or two of them complaining about how late it was, a few outbursts of not too enthusiastic laughter. Then Mr. Fusari was introducing him. It was time. He turned and walked quickly up to the speaker's table, shook hands once more with Mr. Fusari, and then looked out at the teachers waiting for him to begin.

"I hope you are feeling experimental today," he said, "and I hope you don't mind being guinea pigs for the next half hour or so. Now I understand that you've been looking at the issue of grading here at West High during the past few days, and I'd like to put you and this computer (he patted the strange-looking machine beside him) to work on that subject for a few calculated experiments. Okay?"

A few groans came from the audience, and one or two of the teachers started to whisper to each other. Dr. Miller turned his eyes to the plywood lectern and studied the rather lively four-letter words carved into the surface. He smiled at the idea of reading out a few of them to the teachers to grab their attention. Instead, he waited a few seconds more, marveling at how some teachers could, without embarrassment, act just as they told their own students not to act.

"I'm going to give each of you one of these cards," he continued, holding up a handful of computer cards, "and then I'm going to ask some questions concerning your attitudes toward grading. We'll find out pretty quickly where you stand on the issue."

The A-V crew, finished with the overhead projector, had already started passing out the cards and special pencils. When the job was finished, they left the room.

Dr. Miller flashed on a transparency of the IBM card. "You'll notice," he said, "that there is no place for your name. This is so you'll be as honest as possible without intimidating yourself or anyone else. There's room for 20 answers on the card, as you can see, but I'm only going to ask 10 questions now. When we're done I'll run the cards through the computer. While they're being tabulated, I have another experiment which I think you'll find just as interesting. For that one I'll need all of you to sit with your own departments. And so after everyone is finished, please shift accordingly."

Dr. Miller turned back to the screen and explained that each of the questions required the teachers to consider a factor which they believed should or should not influence grading. "For example," he said, replacing the first transparency with the second one, "I might ask whether you think a student's race should affect his grade. You answer by coloring in one of the five possible replies printed on the card." His finger projected large and black on the screen and touched the scale to which he was referring:

Transparency No. 2—Scale To Be Used

A. It would be very important to consider this item when grading.
B. Somewhat important.
C. I have no strong feelings either way.
D. Should not be considered very heavily when grading.
E. Definitely should not be considered at all when grading.

"Should we answer that last question?" someone asked.

"No," said Dr. Miller quickly. And then, by shaking his head and crossing his forefinger against his lips, he indicated that the time for talking was over.

"Number one," he said, in a much louder and more impersonal manner, "Do you think a student's I.Q. should be taken into consideration in his grade?" He had written each question out on separate transparencies and he placed each of them on the projector in the order in which he asked them.

"Number two," he continued. "Should final exams be taken into consideration when grading at the end of the semester?"

"Number three: Do you think weekly quizzes should be used? By that," he clarified, "I mean one quiz a week, whether it is surprise or scheduled, but with perfect regularity."

"Four: Where do you stand on a monthly test—or at least one large test for each marking period?"

"Five: Should a student's popularity with other students enter into the grade?"

The young professor paused then and waited for the slower teachers (or perhaps the more contemplative ones) to catch up. Periodically, one or two of them glanced up at the screen or chewed nervously at the ends of pencils before marking the cards in front of them.

"Number six: Should class participation be considered in the grade?" And then quickly . . . "Seven: Is the student's social class a factor? Eight: Should the student's ability to give you back exactly the same answers you want be considered? (A few ironic giggles rippled across the room, but Dr. Miller kept going.) Nine: Should the student's ability to take issue with what you say, to argue and sometimes to prove you wrong, be considered? (More giggles. A sigh. A groan.) And the last one: Where do you stand on the idea of a curve? I mean on the premise that there should be an equal number of people receiving low and high grades?"

The screen contained all 10 questions now, in addition to the rating scale, and Dr. Miller gave the teachers a few more seconds to check their answers before he called for the cards.

Mr. Ingles scraped his chair against the hardwood floor and joined the other teachers moving around the room to gather with the people from their own departments. He glanced at his watch, shook his head, and thought about the lawn he would not be mowing that afternoon. At least it was not a straight lecture—at least there was something to do, he mused to himself as he joined his fellow science instructors. They were all sitting and discussing their answers, but Mr. Ingles remained silent.

"Through the light-fingered efforts of some of my students," Dr. Miller was saying, "I have obtained some actual test papers written by students from other high schools in the city. Now these have been duplicated, and I'm going to give all members of each department a copy of the same paper. You grade the paper as if it had been written especially for you. The idea, of course, is to see just how close your marks will be to those of your colleagues."

Mr. Crewson and Mr. Fusari were already passing out the papers and red pencils. "Any predictions?" Dr. Miller queried softly.

Mr. Ingles seemed to come to life for the first time that afternoon. His hand shot up. "I'll bet that the English teachers have a spread of 30 or more points, but those of us in math and sciences will be as close as five points straight down the line." Mr. Ingles was grinning and his associates around him were nodding their heads. Not a word came from the English Department. Mr. Ingles grinned even more.

Smiling, Dr. Miller said: "Are you ready? Remember, consider this test paper a real one and grade it as you would if it belonged to any one of your students." He paused for a second, smiled once more, and continued with his instructions: "Eyes on your own paper. Do your own work."

The large room grew silent; only the sounds of turning pages and the efficient clicking of the little computer could be heard. Outside a truck passed. A car horn blared.

"Finish up now," Dr. Miller's sharp voice sliced through the silence. "Actually, I've given you about twice the time you would take if you had a whole stack of papers in front of you."

There were a few *sotto voce* remarks as the teachers placed pencils on the table and sat upright once more.

"Put a grade on the paper," Dr. Miller told them, "but not your name, and hand them in face down. One person from each table please collect them and trade them for a batch from a table not in your subject matter."

Mr. Ingles' table had traded with the English Department. "Hey," he said loudly, looking over the paper he had been handed. "Somebody in English misspelled *commitment* in his marginal notes."

Dr. Miller interrupted the laughter almost before it started. It was getting late and he still had quite a lot to do. "Okay. Since English seems to be considered so vulnerable, let's hear the spread of grades you gave that essay question paper on *Macbeth*."

He asked for the hands of those people holding English papers. He nodded. Then he asked for hands of people with English papers graded below 70 or "C." Two went up. "What were the actual grades?"

"I have 68," one teacher said from the back of the room.

"This one has a large 'C' with a small minus circled in blue ink." It was Miss Doyle. "Maybe it means one is for content and one is for grammar."

"You get an 'A'," someone from the English table quipped.

"Okay, hold on," Dr. Miller called for quiet. Then he asked for people with an English paper with an "A" or with 90 or more. Three more hands went up.

"Aha! What did I tell you," Mr. Ingles said triumphantly, now very much interested in what was going on.

"What are the actual grades and comments?" Dr. Miller asked.

" 'A—Very thought-provoking.' "

" 'Couldn't agree with you less,' " came the second answer, " 'but I admire the way you put it.' "

"I've got an even better one than that," said a third teacher, " 'A— and B— equal B+.' "

"That's separate grading for grammar and content, then figured together," someone said stonily from the English Department. No one looked too happy there.

"Well now," said Dr. Miller slowly, pacing back and forth in front of the lectern, "who is right and who is wrong? Is it an 'A' paper or a 'C' paper? Or is it somewhere in between? And for that matter," he continued, "what would have happened if you had known the student? And what if this were the 35th paper you read at one sitting instead of the first? And perhaps even more relevant, would the grade have been the same, say, if this were a Monday instead of a Friday? I wonder . . ."

"Look, Dr. Miller," Mr. Ingles stood up quickly. He was no longer smiling. "You may be making some points where it concerns the English Department, but I'd like to see the spread among the science papers if you don't mind."

The professor nodded. "Okay. I suppose that's a fair request. Let's do it with a show of hands. How many science papers were marked lower than 'C,' 69 or under?" he asked. Two hands went up. "Between 70 and 79?" Two more hands. "Over 90?" One hand.

"Why, this is ridiculous," Mr. Ingles shot up again. "I don't believe it. There are only seven of us in the department and that paper deserved a solid 'B.' "

"You're crazy," Cliff Harper stood up and faced him. "Just because the kid has the right answers doesn't mean he knows how he got them. Unless a student goes through the entire process, I take off points. Doesn't everybody?"

"I don't know about everybody," Mr. Ingles sputtered back, his face turning pink. "I only know about me. I don't worry about cheating or about collecting scrap paper. I worry about whether a student has a right answer or a wrong one, and this kid did the job."

The debate between the two science teachers was drowned out by a hubbub of controversy that had erupted around the room. Dr. Miller allowed the teachers to argue among themselves a bit longer as he said something in Mr. Crewson's ear. Mr. Crewson nodded, then Dr. Miller walked back and slammed his fist on the table for quiet.

"Hold on now," he said. "It's quite obvious that grades mean different things to different people—even in the so-called objective disciplines like math and science. Now let's try one more experiment before we call it a day."

He didn't wait for comments. He asked the teachers to get out a piece of scrap paper and put numbers on it from one to 10.

"This is a quiz," he said, "and may be used to determine your next salary increase."

Mr. Ingles glared up at the professor, along with a few other teachers. This time there was no laughter. Dr. Miller ignored the hostile faces and launched right into the questions. "Question one: What is a standard deviation?"

"You must be kidding," Miss Doyle said loudly.

He was not kidding.

"Question two: Explain what a mean is. Three: Define median. Four: What is a normal distribution? Five: What is a reliable test?"

Mr. Ingles threw down his pencil. "This is ridiculous," he said. "What's he trying to do?" His face had now turned a glowing red. Dr. Miller ignored the remark and the groans and sighs of disgust. Inexorably, he asked his questions in a cold and confident staccato.

"What is validity? What is objectivity? List the measurements you use to determine the reliability of one of your own tests. How do you know that the last quiz you gave was valid? And finally, tell me please— just tell me—what right you have to grade other people's children."

The room was silent as Dr. Miller looked out across the plywood lectern at the West High faculty. He wanted to look at their eyes, he wanted to ask them these questions again and again until he got his answer, the only answer that they could possibly give. But no one—not one teacher—would look back at him. Fingernails were being studied. Desks and papers and the floor were under examination. And looking out at those hiding faces, Dr. Miller was angry.

He had told himself that he would be cold and scientific and calculating, that he would try to be objective and understanding and impersonal. But he was also angry. He was vitally concerned with the way these people in this room on this Friday would from now on confront the problems of evaluating their students.

"I suppose I should apologize," he said finally in a very soft and controlled tone, "for the harsh way I asked those questions. But my own objectivity, where grading is concerned, is sometimes very strained. You see, grades to you are just incidental letters and numbers, but to students—especially students today—grades mean much more. Don't you see?"

He walked around the table toward the faculty, "Grades can and often do determine who is sent to Vietnam; grades can systematically screen out lower-income children from getting some of the benefits that their more wealthy peers take for granted.

"I think that there's nothing—nothing that more effectively separates students and teachers—that drives them actually into warring camps—than grades. The student has his crib sheets, his rote memorization, his apple polishing. Teachers combat these devices with Mickey Mouse assignments, surprise quizzes, notebook checks, tricky multiple-choice questions.

"Grades have made us into overseers driving the most reluctant group of field hands ever known. Grades have made us puppeteers pulling the emotional strings of live marionettes. Grades have made our students believe that 'wadjaget' is the most important word to be used when summarizing their own education."

Dr. Miller turned and walked quickly to the miniature computer. He picked up the printout and held it in his hand without looking down at it.

"I think there are serious problems in this high school—as there are in so many other high schools—problems that both teachers and administrators need to face. We can see it in this printout," he said, pointing down at the long white sheet coming from the machine. "I see a tremendous spread of opinion about which kinds of things should be considered in grading.

"Take Question Seven," he continued. "More than 80 percent of you said that social class should not be considered when grading. And yet you are all aware that students in the general section of this high school are there because of their social class. You justify not putting them into college entrance sections on the grounds that they are too lazy or that they supposedly cannot read. Those general students have been neatly 'classed out' of the rewards of this school and you and teachers like you have done it to them.

"Let's go to Question Eight. 'Should the student's ability to give you back exactly the answers you want to hear be considered in his grade?' Ninety-five percent of you said that it should not be given much weight; it should definitely not be considered when grading. But I wonder. Do your students have this understanding?

"I recently interviewed 50 of your students in the context of a research on student dissent I am doing. I am convinced—*I was told*—that students think that not giving *your* answer—the answer they think you want—leads to a lower grade. You may not have tried to do it, but that's what you have accomplished. 'Give them what they want to hear,' your students say of you, 'and do it neatly, without erasures.'"

Suddenly Dr. Miller felt very weary. His suitcoat, the bright library lights, even the weight of the printout in his hand seemed to put unbearable pressure on his arms and shoulders.

"I'll leave this printout with Mr. Fusari," he said quietly, "and I'm hoping that he'll want to call another meeting about this topic in the near future. Thank you very much for your time and attention."

Changing the Grading Game:
A Chronology of Progress and Pitfalls

James B. Van Hoven

IN SEPTEMBER OF 1970, the teachers and administrators of Briarcliff Manor Middle School, Briarcliff, New York, agreed that reporting practices must come into line with the school's instructional philosophy and practices. From that initial decision came a three-year struggle which combined the wishes of the faculty, the wants of parents, and the needs of students into a reporting system which continues to evolve.

The history of the change which occurred during the 1970–1973 school years is outlined here. The change process, as adopted by the administration and faculty, provided the framework for each year. These were the major steps taken:

• Identify staff and community assumptions. The assumptions could include hopes, fears, attitudes, or values of parents and staff;

• Take action which will consider all assumptions;

• Measure reaction;

• Develop strategies to support positive reaction and correct causes of negative reaction;

• Implement as board policy the best attributes of change.

As one scrutinizes the history of change in the middle school's reporting system, one should recognize the following:

• Change does not come swiftly or strongly, but through a slow evolution which involves all persons—school professionals and community—in the decision-making process.

126

• Change is not a win-lose game. It is compromise in the search for the best results, those which satisfy sometimes conflicting needs.

• Grading changes do not occur in an instructional vacuum. Grades, report cards, or other evaluation instruments must coincide with the instructional practices of the school.

1970-71

I. Strategies for Change

A. Staff

Assumption #1: Reporting practices and instructional strategies are mutually interdependent.

Assumption #2: Therefore, a change in one should necessitate a change in the other.

Assumption #3: Changes in both are necessary in order to humanize and individualize instruction.

The staff identified and agreed on the need to change reporting practices. Therefore, practices were changed *before or while* changes in instructional strategy began. These changes then affected the direction of instructional change.

B. Community

Assumption #1: Adequate information, rationally presented, can persuade people to accept change.

Assumption #2: Parents desire more information about their student's progress.

II. Action

Traditional letter grades were eliminated and replaced with a system involving:
• Checklists in each subject area reflecting important behavioral outcomes for students; student ratings on a five-point scale for each area relative to the school's perception of his/her potential.
• Narrative reports (two per year per subject).
• Parent conferences (two per year).

III. Reaction

A. Staff began to individualize and humanize education and became committed to continue progress toward these goals.

B. Many parents were confused or hostile to changes, claiming that competition was essential in schools, that colleges required grades, and that the school was too soft.

C. Some parents polled the community informally and found overwhelming interest in grades.

IV. Re-reaction

A. A parent-teacher group was formed to poll the community scientifically.

B. The principal organized community coffee-hours to explain school programs.

C. The scientific poll noted above indicated that most parents accepted the changes made.

D. The principal and staff concluded that progress-related "potential" was inappropriate and that rather, progress should be relative to instructional objectives.

V. Final Action

A. The board of education required a modification of the Pupil Progress Report to reflect a student's standing relative to his or her peers (at, above, or below grade level).

B. The board of education endorsed the concept noted in Section IV, D, above and directed the staff and principal to clearly define the objectives of instruction for all subjects. As this was done, the checklists (Pupil Progress Reports) would be phased out.

1971-72

I. Strategies for Change

A. Staff

Assumption #1: It would be relatively easy to define instructional objectives for all subject areas as well as appropriate learning activities.

Assumption #2: Reporting progress relative to student potential is an improvement over past practices, but is not as appropriate as reporting student progress relative to instructional objectives.

B. Community

Assumption #1: Most people in the community have accepted the new procedures.

Assumption #2: People can only take so much change; a low profile is now needed.

II. Action

A. Numerous workshops were held with staff members to inform them about instructional objectives and how to identify them.

B. The reporting system continued as modified at the end of the previous year.

C. A staff committee met in the spring to review the next steps regarding reporting.

III. Reaction

A. Most staff members reacted adversely to the identification of instructional objectives because:

1. Instructional objectives can best be identified only in areas that are sequential and/or cognitive.
2. This approach came to be seen as being in conflict with humanization.
3. It raised the issue of staff accountability.

4. More work was required.

5. It was a new idea.

B. Since no visible changes in the reporting system were made, the community remained silent.

C. The faculty committee recommended:

1. Minor changes in the dates and times of conferences.

2. Minor changes in the content of the checklists.

3. The establishment of a parent-teacher committee to examine, in depth, the reporting system.

IV. Final Action

A. The board of education permitted minor changes in the content of the checklist, but did not permit changes in the dates of reporting, since the staff had not completed the task of developing instructional objectives. It directed the principal to continue to pursue this objective.

B. A parent-teacher committee was formed to look at the whole process the following year.

1972-73

I. Strategies for Change

A. Staff

Assumption #1: Most issues are not "either/or," "black or white." Identifying and sequencing instructional objectives, where *possible* is not inconsistent with humanistic goals.

Assumption #2: People learn the above by having increased information and working through problems together.

B. Community

Assumption #1: A group of parents and teachers representing all ranges of opinion, by being better informed and by working through problems together, will achieve consensus that a reporting system linked to general instructional objectives should be implemented.

II. Action

A. Staff, through increased sophistication and work in individualization, began in some areas to identify and sequence instructional objectives (for math, English, social studies skills, foreign language, and science in particular).

B. The parent-teacher committee, with polarized parent representatives (screaming liberals and arch conservatives), fought like tigers. The committee's final report was very general with few recommendations, but contained the observation that there was apparently "little dissatisfaction" with the middle school reporting system. The report reinforced the feeling that reporting based on student potential was inappropriate.

As of this date, an equilibrium has been established among parents and teachers regarding reporting. Neither group is entirely happy with the present system. The staff will not move back to a traditional system

MARKING CODE

BASED ON THE STUDENT'S ACADEMIC POTENTIAL

VG-VERY GOOD   G-GOOD   S-SATISFACTORY   U-UNSATISFACTORY
X-NOT APPLICABLE

ATTENDANCE	1	2	3	4
DAYS ABSENT				
DAYS TARDY				

STUDENT _____

GRADE _____

ADVISOR _____

SUBJECT	QUARTER			
LANGUAGE ARTS	I	II	III	IV
BASIC UNDERSTANDING IN READING				
ABILITY TO INTERPRET LITERATURE				
MECHANICS & ORGANIZATION OF WRITING				
CREATIVITY IN WRITING				
ORAL PARTICIPATION				
SELF-RELIANCE IN INDEPENDENT STUDY				
COMPLETES ASSIGNMENTS				
SHOWS POSITIVE ATTITUDE				

SUBJECT	QUARTER			
FOREIGN LANGUAGE	I	II	III	IV
PRESENTLY STUDYING UNIT:				
RATE OF PROGRESS				
WORK HABITS				
RELATIONS WITH OTHERS				
RESEARCH (CIVILIZATION)				
PROJECT EXECUTION (CIVILIZATION)				
LISTENING COMPREHENSION				
READING COMPREHENSION				
GRAMMAR CONCEPTS				
PRONUNCIATION & INTONATION				
ORAL RESPONSE				
SPELLING				
SENTENCE FORMATION				

SUBJECT	QUARTER			
MUSIC	I	II	III	IV
SHOWS COMPREHENSION OF COURSE CONTENT				
SHOWS ABILITY TO LISTEN WITH UNDERSTANDING				
SHOWS ABILITY TO SING ON PITCH				
TAKES PART IN CLASS ACTIVITIES				
USES MUSIC FOR SELF EXPRESSION				

SUBJECT	QUARTER			
MATHEMATICS	I	II	III	IV
HAS COMPLETED ASSIGNMENT NUMBER:				
RATE OF PROGRESS				
ABILITY TO GENERALIZE & APPLY MATH CONCEPTS				
COMPUTATION SKILLS				
WORD PROBLEM SOLVING				
INTERPRETS & FOLLOWS DIRECTIONS				
DEMONSTRATES PERSEVERANCE				
WORKS WELL INDEPENDENTLY				
IS COOPERATIVE WITH STUDENTS				
IS COOPERATIVE WITH TEACHER				

SUBJECT	QUARTER			
PHYSICAL EDUCATION	I	II	III	IV
CLASS ATTITUDE AND BEHAVIOR				
PERSISTENT EFFORT IN WORKING TO CAPACITY				
MOTOR COORDINATION SKILLS				
ABILITY TO WORK INDEPENDENTLY				

HEALTH (GRADE 7)	I	II	III	IV

UNIFIED ARTS	I	II	III	IV
ART				
USES ART MEDIA TO EXPRESS PERSONAL THOUGHTS AND FEELING				
KNOWLEDGE & APPLICATION OF PRINCIPLES & ELEMENTS OF DESIGN				
SKILL & CRAFTSMANSHIP WITH MATERIALS				
EXPERIMENTS WITH MATERIALS & SOLVES PROBLEMS INDEPENDENTLY				
WORKS WELL WITH OTHERS				

INDUSTRIAL ARTS				
TOOL KNOWLEDGE & APPLICATION				
UNDERSTANDING & USE OF MATERIALS				
PRIDE IN WORKMANSHIP				
COOPERATIVE WORKER WITHIN LABORATORY SETTING				
MANUAL DEXTERITY				

HOME ECONOMICS				
UNDERSTANDS, APPLIES & EVALUATES CONCEPTS				
ORGANIZES, FOLLOWS DIRECTIONS & MANAGES RESOURCES				
ASSUMES RESPONSIBILITY				
CONTRIBUTES TO PERSONAL & GROUP GOALS				

SUBJECT	QUARTER			
SOCIAL STUDIES	I	II	III	IV
UNDERSTANDS MAIN CONCEPTS				
SHOWS ABILITY TO READ & INTERPRET MATERIALS				
PARTICIPATES IN & CONTRIBUTES TO SMALL GROUP ACTIVITIES				
PARTICIPATES IN & CONTRIBUTES TO CLASS ACTIVITIES				
RESPECTS & IS INTERESED IN WORK OF OTHERS				
COMPLETES ASSIGNMENTS PROMPTLY				
COMPLETES ASSIGNMENTS THOROUGHLY				
USES INDEPENDENT STUDY TIME EFFICIENTLY				
ORGANIZES MATERIALS EFFECTIVELY				
ACHIEVES GOALS OF INDEPENDENT STUDY				

SUBJECT	QUARTER			
SCIENCE	I	II	III	IV
(GRADES 7 & 8) CHAPTERS COMPLETED:				
RATE OF PROGRESS				
KNOWLEDGE OF FUNDAMENTAL CONCEPTS				
ABILITY TO READ & INTERPRET DATA				
APPLICATION TO NEW SITUATIONS				
WORKS INDEPENDENTLY WITH RESPONSIBILITY				
SHOWS HONESTY & SINCERITY IN INVESTIGATIONS				
SHOWS PROPER LABORATORY TECHNIQUE				
SHOWS ABILITY TO COMMUNICATE ORALLY & IN WRITING				

GRADE LEVEL PERFORMANCE	I	II	III	IV
1 - ABOVE GRADE LEVEL				
2 - AT GRADE LEVEL				
3 - BELOW GRADE LEVEL				
LANGUAGE ARTS				
MATHEMATICS				
SOCIAL STUDIES				
SCIENCE				
FOREIGN LANGUAGE (_____)				

	I	II	III	IV
GENERAL SCHOOL CITIZENSHIP				

S - SATISFACTORY   U - UNSATISFACTORY

nor would the community as a whole want to. On the other hand, the staff has not achieved the goal of sequencing all appropriate instructional objectives and activities, although some notable progress has been made. The community would probably welcome such a development, since it has a clear, rational base and since community members are quite well informed about the issues involved.

In summary, the existent system continues to report on the basis of student potential, using conferences, narratives, and checklists. Despite this obvious flaw, the following advantages have accrued:

• The concept of failure has practically been eliminated from the system.

• Communication between the school and parents regarding pupil progress has been vastly increased through the conferences and narratives.

• All the misinterpretations and inaccuracies of the older system of single letter grades were eliminated.

• The staff members have recognized the importance of instructional objectives and appropriate learning activities and have continued to develop and refine their individualized programs.

The Principal Looks at Grading Changes

William J. Bailey

IF YOU ARE a principal or if you know one, you are aware that principals receive considerable criticism for almost everything they do. On the other hand, you should be aware that a principal is often the key person in bringing about significant changes in education. Bringing about change, however, can polarize many people.

One area in which the principal is sure to polarize opinions is that of grading system changes. Surveys have shown and logic tells us that making a change in the grading system is extremely difficult, something like trying to move a cemetery—a change that causes many people to get excited.

However high the risks, the thinking principal must continually examine and revise the student evaluation system. Evaluation is crucial to student progress and is a significant part of teachers' instructional strategies; it is also an important component of organizational growth and prosperity. If the building principal thinks that conventional grades, with their normative connotations, are "degrading" to students or at least inadequate measures, then he or she should examine many alternatives and start the change and/or revision process.

This chapter will delineate some relatively [1] safe ways to change the grading system. It is based, in part, on the author's specific experiences at Concord High School in Wilmington, Delaware, where significant changes were made; and it is also based on a variety of internal and external consultative experiences in grades 1-12.

[1] Interpreted as "avoiding being fired."

132

Change Agentry

Leslie This,[2] in *A Guide to Effective Management*, points out that change can be either proactive or reactive. Applying this concept to grading changes, one would think that if the principal waits for other schools to change; for parents to complain; for lawsuits to arise from accountability concerns; for alternative education groups to apply pressure; or for other external forces to emerge, then he or she can be said to be "reactive." The reactive change agent may facilitate the change; but there is a tendency for him or her to lose control over the outcome, for the project to be done piecemeal, and for the product to be incongruent with the original intent.

The "proactive" principal, who acts as a change agent, plans for the change in a positive way and thus, gains greater control over the outcomes. This inside-out process initiated by the proactive principal is necessary for accomplishing changes in the grading process. The task is complex and needs careful planning.

There are two modes of change "tracks" for altering the grading system. One is the radical approach, which might be used by students or revisionist faculty groups because both are normally removed from the power source. The proactive principal is close to the power source, by definition, and thus can use conventional management methods of change. These include regular techniques of communication within organizations such as memorandums, position papers, reports, meetings, committees and task forces, seminars, pilot studies, and others.

Structures, Processes, Attitudes

Once the proactive principal, using conventional means of influence, begins thinking, he or she needs a plan of action. One very effective concept of social change, called the SPA formula, has been developed by Goodwin Watson.[3] Briefly, this entails social engineering. It first calls for a change in *structures* (S), which in turn causes people to alter *processes* (P) of operation and behavior, which then gives people a chance to develop a change in *attitudes* (A). This can be a very helpful concept from an organizational point of view, in that a group must

[2] Leslie E. This. *A Guide to Effective Management*. Reading, Massachusetts: Addison-Wesley Publishing Company, Inc., 1974. p. 187.

[3] Goodwin Watson, editor. *Change in School Systems*. Washington, D.C.: Cooperative Project for Education Development, National Training Laboratories, National Education Association, 1967. p. 25.

experience a normative attitude change in accepting innovation, if proper and lasting implementation is to occur. An example of this concept follows.

As principal of Concord High School where radical grading changes took place, I initiated changes in basic structures. Specific changes included individualized learning strategies, mini-courses, self-paced instructional materials, independent study, team teaching, liberal drop-add policies, varied time intervals for grade reporting periods, pass/fail courses, liberal "incomplete" policies, nongradedness, the use of learning recycling patterns, and eventually, the dropping of failing grades (E).

All of these structural changes began to expose the inadequacies of conventional normative grading. They caused teachers to look at their practices of reporting student progress in a different light. Two examples of this were that: (a) teachers (team teaching) began to share their grading practices; and (b) the self-paced learning strategies made it difficult to use the "curve." In effect, we began to see changes and alterations in process behavior—in the procedural operations of evaluating.

Once people began to behave in a different manner, they began to change their values and their attitudes about students, student achievement, and the grading system.

Compliance, Identification, Internalization

Another "formula" that may prove useful in effecting change is based on *compliance, identification,* and *internalization* (CII).[4] I view this as a helpful awareness of the personal, internal process of change that parallels the SPA organizational or group change. In other words, the first sign of change for an individual is based on his instinctual needs to conform or comply. The boss or some program edict has pressured at least some minimal overt changes. Although these changes are at first superficial, the individual's motivation to conform becomes an important incentive in making the grading changes. There is a general need to "get in line," at least with minor changes, because "a school should be consistent."

The next thing that can happen is a psychological process involving "needs of identity." Peer and program identity can be a significant motive in bringing about permanent change. New ideas and programs receive notoriety and attract attention. Even if the attention is negative, it can serve to bring a staff together and lead staff members to identify

[4] Herbert C. Kelman. "Compliance, Identification, and Internalization: Three Processes of Attitude Change." *Journal of Conflict Resolution* 2(1): 51-60; 1958.

with the cause. The proactive principal must watch for these signs and use them constructively.

The individual change that can then occur is internalization: The individual has first conformed, then identified with, and now fully believes in the idea. At the internalized stage, he or she will be glad to defend the new grading system in public. This formula of CII is not seen by this administrator as a social engineering device, but rather as a developmental pattern for which awareness is helpful.

Social Engineering

There are, however, definite change strategies, classified as social engineering, that can be used in making grading changes. If the term social engineering bothers you, then remember that this method of change does not have to be manipulative (secret), as the principal can be very open and honest about its use.

Social engineering strategies one might employ can be categorized as: economic, authoritative, fellowship, rational/logical, ethical, and political.[5] The categorical terms are somewhat self-explanatory, but examples might be helpful.

A model of the economic strategy was demonstrated at Concord High School when the school was able to receive a Title III Grant to implement a proposal for an alternative grading system. The grant reinforced the professionals who were eager for the change, encouraged those who previously had been reluctant, and convinced some members of the critical public of the credibility of the project. Of course, the money was helpful in developing content through in-service workshops, but the strategy was very effective in terms of facilitating the change. In this case, the result was a performance-based, criterion-referenced system.

Another important strategy, which is part of the fellowship category, lies in developing support groups. At Concord it worked in the following way. As principal, I made friends with several of the informal leaders in the school and over many cups of coffee in a variety of settings, we developed a mutual feeling of trust, and shared values about student evaluations. This nucleus eventually spread to a larger group whose members became convinced there was something *we* could do. Their influence on the more reluctant ones was immeasurably helpful in implementing the actual change.

Politically, this support group convinced enough of the staff so

[5] Adapted from Kurt E. Olmosk. "Seven Pure Strategies of Change." In: John Jones and William Pfeiffer, editors. *The 1972 Handbook for Group Facilitators*. La Jolla, California: University Associates, 1972.

that at a crucial moment when a faculty vote was taken, the new approach was accepted. Without this political influence, the plan could not have been implemented. It could be said that because of political influences the faculty normative behavior became one of acceptance.

Planning

The key to all change strategies is planning. There are many models available to the proactive principal, but in all cases, one preplanning decision must be made. In the beginning, the initiator of any idea prior to any announcements of that idea, must make some decisions about the level of involvement. This level of involvement, as a preplanning device, can be viewed on a continuum as seen below.

Level of Involvement

Quality				Compromise			Involvement		
1	2	3	4	5	6	7	8	9	10

At the lower numbered levels is the position of "quality." Quality is defined here as the principal's "perfect plan"—the model the principal wants or dreams about. If magic wands were on the low-bid list we could simply install this quality model. Such a unilateral change, however, produces low implementation impact because those affected by the grading change (parents, students, and teachers) are not involved in the decision making. Assuming the principal is the expert and can devise a real quality alternative to grading, it won't be much good if it cannot withstand the pressure of implementation and operation.

On the other side of the involvement continuum is complete involvement of students, parents, teachers, school board, committees, task forces, and study groups, coupled with input from pilot studies, seminars, and surveys. Of course, there is the old joke about the camel being invented by a committee. The end product may be something entirely different from what the principal had in mind. All of this involvement, as a matter of fact, will probably kill the idea before it has a chance. *However, the greater the involvement, the greater is the chance of implementation and permanency.* More participation will mean more acceptance.

The proactive principal, then, very early in the change process, must make some judgments about involvement. Usually a compromise placing the involvement level between 4-6 on the scale is workable. Placement too far to the right will mean destruction of the ideas as conceived, and placement too far to the left will mean extreme difficulties in making the ideas operational.

Once the principal is aware of this concept, he or she can proceed with planning, which should follow systematic procedures to some degree. One plan that has been used is as follows:

Defining the problem: The present grading system is inadequate when used to evaluate an individualized and nongraded curriculum.

Collecting the data:
Percentages of failures
Percentages of failures in sophisticated courses such as calculus
Student morale
Student discipline at grading time
Student resentment of honor rolls and honor societies
Evidence of cheating
Teacher dissatisfaction
Drop-add lists
Counseling feedback
Parental complaints
Research about grades and job performance

Establishing alternatives:
Mastery-performance
Written-anecdotal
Pass-fail
No evaluation at all
Self-evaluations
Credit-no credit
Combinations

Selecting one alternative course of action: Install a mastery-performance system of grading.

Implementing that course of action: In a large high school this can be delegated to teams or departments when they are ready. At Concord, implementation occurred when we had developed the course objectives to use as criteria for mastery.

Research and studies show that the principal (manager) of a school or institution does have an effect on the organization and on the organization's constituents. The proactive principal can set the climate that is conducive to change and can initiate the structural changes necessary to start a change action process. The proactive principal *can* develop a planning scheme. Grades must "go" because they fail the educational system; the proactive principal must be the one to create that change. This is the real role of change agentry.

In Conclusion:
Dispelling the Grading Myths

Richard L. Curwin

I RECENTLY ATTENDED a meeting of college administrators and faculty members who were considering a request (initiated by a student committee representing about one-third of the total enrollment) to reform their grading policy. The strongest and most influential argument against the request was that it would cost too much money to change the computer from the traditional A-B-C-D-E system to a Credit/No Credit system. In essence, this argument, in conjunction with strong anti-reform sentiment, was enough to destroy the chances for adoption of the students' request. Reflecting on this event, I feel that if the needs of the computer are more influential and important than the needs of students in dictating educational policy, then perhaps talk of grading reform is too late. We have been dehumanized to the point of loving machines more than people.

However, I really don't think that it is too late. Certainly, the mechanistic grading systems in our public and private institutions of learning are disheartening. But grading change can occur and has occurred in the past, and it appears that a new movement is under way. It is ironic that there is a current national thrust to move away from traditional grading systems concurrent with a thrust to move toward performance-, competency-, and accountability-based programs. These two seemingly opposite thrusts are more closely allied than is apparent at first glance.

The reason for the apparent discrepancy is the abundance of widespread myths that are considered truths about grading. These myths are, in effect, preventing grading reform and are, as Arthur W. Combs says, filled with half-truths (in some cases quarter- or eighth-truths). They are, therefore, hard to dislodge. Consider four of these myths.

Weighing the Half-Truths

First Myth: Learning requires evaluation: By eliminating grading, you also eliminate evaluation. This conviction, as I learned in introductory logic, consists of two parts; the truth of the second part is validated by the truth of the first. In other words, the only way that this myth can be true is if grading is evaluation, or the best evaluation; but grading is, in fact, one of the poorest methods of evaluation, if it evaluates at all. Good evaluation systems must provide information for students—information that indicates what they have done well, what areas of their performance are in need of modification, and what areas are in need of improvement. Good evaluation supplies data for students to make decisions about their lives. It comments upon student skills, interests, knowledge, and reflects the instructor's understanding of each individual's unique characteristics. For evaluation to be useful, it must be informative, unique, and substantive. Global generalizations such as grades prove to be more harmful than beneficial in the education process. They allow students, teachers, parents, and others to draw false, blanket conclusions.

Those who use letter grades are locked into vague generalizations. What does a B tell a student about his progress? Certainly nothing that can help him change and grow. A grade of B tells a student that his performance has been judged better, *from the perceptions of the teacher,* than the performances of students who received C's and not as well as the work of those who received A's. If a teacher uses a curve for the determination of grades, the B could mean even less. Thus, if a teacher uses *only* grades to supply feedback to students, that teacher is doing his students a disservice by stifling the learning process. Few teachers, however, use only grades. Most supply other kinds of both formal and informal evaluation and feedback. Without evaluation, grades are meaningless; with evaluation, they are unnecessary. Obviously educators need to spend more time developing and implementing better feedback and evaluation devices which are more useful to the learner.

Second Myth: Grades are motivators; they push students to do their best. It is true that grades help motivate students, but motivate them to what?—to get good grades, of course. This means, in effect, that given a choice between learning and getting a good grade, the majority of students choose, almost without exception, the good grade. A powerful illustration is the rise in term paper companies, which are now multi-million-dollar enterprises. While these businesses are fairly new on the educational scene, the principle behind them has been in operation for years in dormitory, fraternity, and sorority filing systems for term papers and exams.

Yet there is a worse side effect from grades. It is the deadening of learning that looms as the most tragic consequence. There is a strong probability that the "poor-grade getter" will become a poor learner. Studies have demonstrated the power of the self-fulfilling prophecy on both the teacher and the student, showing that as a student receives poor grades, his self-concept is lowered. Further research has demonstrated that self-concept is perhaps one of the strongest, single influences in learning. Any aspect of the teaching-learning cycle that diminishes self-concept, therefore, must diminish learning potential. The effect, then, of a poor grade is not to make the student try harder the next time, as many people claim, but to weaken the student's learning ability. We only need to look at the continuing record of failure—a record which for so many students never breaks—to realize that the research speaks accurately.

What about the "good-grade getters"? Do they become better learners? Actually, those who receive good grades are reinforced to keep on receiving good grades. Good grades become more important to students who have accepted the notion that good grades mean good self-worth. Even the students who are perceptive enough to see through this façade recognize that the key to their future might rest on their grade laurels and most are willing to pay the price. What happens is that students who get good grades become very adept at playing the grading game. They can "psych" out their teachers with consummate skill and insight. Questions like, "Will this be on the test?" or "Does this count?" and "Am I responsible for this?" are common among the players of the grading game, for their success depends on their ability to give the teacher what he or she wants.

During class discussions those who play the grading game write down only what the teacher says, using the time when another student speaks to rest their hands. They know that no matter how interesting it may be, a student's comment will undoubtedly be excluded from the examination. None of the students who get good grades are willing to jeopardize their chances in the grading game by veering from a successful pattern of behavior.

Students often use the same thinking process when they write essentially the same paper or examination throughout the term, changing it only to fit different contexts. It is highly unlikely that a good-grade getter will ever examine the process of his or her learning, for that can never be rewarded by good grades. Neither will such students be motivated to behave creatively or uniquely. The fact is that grades can only be determined by accounting for the most insignificant aspects of learning. It is impossible to consider, in terms of letter grades, the values, feelings, creativity, intuition, judgment, higher levels of cognitive thinking, or any of the other things that truly influence the lives of students. Thus, students who wish to receive good grades must either ignore, or separate from their work in school, these important yet frequently intangible elements of education, and concentrate instead on what will gain them a reward through the grading system. In this choice of priorities lie the seeds for the "paper chase" so many universities decry, but seem powerless to end. As stated earlier, grades motivate students not to learn, but to get good grades.

Third Myth: Grades are, or can be, objective. Many educators assume that it is possible for them to grade fairly because they are detached, or because they treat all students the same, or because they account for individual differences, or because they use a numerical system, or because of a multitude of other reasons. In actuality, any one system of determining grades is biased because its goals and procedures are based upon the perceptual field of the teacher using it.

We can easily understand this subjectivity by looking at the different criteria teachers use to determine what is worth a good grade. In grading papers or essays, some teachers give points for each correct response covered in the answer; others consider style as an important factor; some teachers count spelling and punctuation; others consider length. I know of a teacher who only reads footnotes in term papers, while another teacher dislikes them and takes off for their too frequent use. In math there are teachers who only give credit for correct answers; others give credit for the correct process even if the answer is incorrect; others take off for careless computation, while others only give credit for use of the proper format. Neatness is often a factor for some teachers, and not a factor for others.

In the traditional grading system, the definition of good work depends upon the purposes of the evaluator, usually the teacher. When these purposes are different from the purposes of the learner, only coincidence can make the evaluation worthwhile for the student. In most cases, the students who perform the best are those who have successfully deduced the teacher's purposes. Even if the teacher has overtly specified his or her purposes, they must still be subjectively evaluated, for it is totally arbitrary to assign performance levels to grade levels. For example, an objective raw score, such as eight-right-out-of-ten, can be an A, B, C, D, or E, with equal justification, by considering subjective variables. The determination of grades from raw scores is made by consensus; in most cases it is a consensus of one person—the teacher.

There are other instances of hidden subjectivity. Take, for example, true/false, multiple choice, or short-answer questions, which at first glance seem to be objective. They are subjective, however, because of the factors of inclusion and exclusion. If I prepare a test on *Hamlet* which I want to be objective, I might ask the students whether they know certain facts. True or false: Rosencranz appears on the stage before Guildenstern? By including this question, I am asserting that I believe its answer to be important to an understanding of the play, or whatever my purpose is for studying *Hamlet*. The question, then, is subjectively determined.

Another example of subtle subjectiveness is the interpretation of apparent objective questions. Take, for example, the case of a colleague's son who was asked, "Does one get to Moscow from Rochester, New York, by traveling east or west?" The student was marked wrong by the IBM scoring device that could not properly interpret his answer, "Either, but west is longer."

Problems of interpretation and inclusion/exclusion are no longer important once the grading system is reformed. Scores become data for the student to interpret according to *his* or *her* purposes. One student might decide that eight-out-of-ten is not the best he or she can do, and might make a goal to do better. Another student in the same class might be proud of that score and work on another aspect of the subject in which he or she is having difficulty. A student might not care that he or she didn't know the order of appearance of Rosencranz and Guildenstern because he or she read the play for different purposes than the teacher who asked that question. A different student might find his or her incorrect answer to that question troubling, because he or she is directing the school play and must know the order of character appearances to do a good job. *A student may discard or accept data according to his or her own purposes only if there is no external reward/punishment system imposed.*

Fourth Myth: Grades are needed as a screening device for colleges, graduate schools, and employers. It is true that many institutions of higher education and businesses use grades to determine acceptance. However, if we look at this situation carefully, we notice that the admissions officer or employer wants a competent, qualified candidate to fill his or her position. Specifically, a qualified candidate is one who has the ability and skills to meet the requirements of the school or job. Obviously every school or job has unique requirements and in order to make an accurate assessment of a candidate's ability, much information is necessary. Otherwise, it becomes far too easy to make costly mistakes. Consider the example of a student who receives a B in student teaching because of a difference in educational philosophy with his or her supervisor. A school might pass this candidate up because of the B even though the candidate's philosophy coincides with that of the school, which has hired an A student with a contrary philosophy.

A good screening device, like a good evaluation system, implies the generation of information meaningful to decision making. Data such as strengths, weaknesses, unique characteristics, compatability with the institution considering the applicant, and other pertinent information must be supplied. Grades alone do not supply the necessary information for a fair assessment. With the inclusion of other data, grades are unnecessary.

Many claim that it takes too long for a teacher or school to prepare a sufficient alternative folder and for screening personnel to review it. Yet, there are some methods of data collection and dissemination that are sophisticated enough to provide better means for screening and yet are practical enough to work. Moreover, it takes a great deal of time and energy to compute grades, if a teacher is diligent. The same time could be better spent in filling out a different type of progress report. In the long run, it is far more efficient to hire the best person for the job or to accept the best student and spend more time in doing so, than it is to use the shorthand of grades with the high risk of making costly mistakes.

Furthermore, not everybody in school is applying for college or the relatively few jobs where grades might make any difference. At a conference discussing grades, employment recruiters from companies in the Rochester, New York, area said that grades were only influential in choosing candidates for a small percentage of their jobs (and they considered grades only in lieu of other information). Thus, it seems unfair that the grading policy of a school be based on the needs of a select population of that school. There is no reason for students who will not go on to college or will not apply for the few jobs that are influenced by grades, to be subjected to the tyranny of grading.

In these days when colleges and universities must actively recruit qualified applicants to fill empty residence halls, admissions officers are more prepared to review applicants who do not submit grades, grade point averages, or rank in class. (Ironically, most of the "prestigious" eastern schools, have always worked in this way; only the myth perpetuated by grade-oriented high school teachers called for normative scores.)

Dispelling the Myths

There are three substantial myth-destroyers which give evidence against the belief that colleges need grades: (a) the official position of the American Association of College Registrars and Admissions Officers (AACRAO); (b) the 1973 survey by the Consortium of Experimenting High Schools; (c) the positive experience of more than 100 high school programs which use descriptive and/or criterion-referenced evaluations.

AACRAO States Position

Headed by a consortium of twenty-five experimental colleges (Johnston, Antioch, Goddard, Hampshire, and others), AACRAO has wrestled with external credit evaluation and non-traditional course evaluations. In 1974, AACRAO established a committee to study non-traditional evaluation. At the same time, it reaffirmed its position that each high school should determine the best evaluation procedures for its students. According to AACRAO, admissions officers, in turn, should recognize evaluation as the high school's responsibility, and give fair review to all applicants by considering their records in whatever form they were transcribed.

Survey by Experimental High Schools

In 1973, the National Consortium of Experimenting High Schools surveyed the 2,600 two- and four-year colleges in the United States. Ninety-seven percent replied to the questionnaire with results that surprised even the survey committee. Less than 5 percent indicated that grades or rank in class were an absolute necessity; 18 percent responded that the admissions office had no policy and could not promise fair review; 77 percent indicated that students whose transcripts provided other designated information would receive "fair and equal review." Written evaluations, computer-printed descriptions, and test scores topped the lists of needed information for four-year colleges. The vast majority of public two-year schools needed only a diploma, or a birth certificate showing the applicant to be at least 18 years old. Individual college responses are catalogued in the *College Guide for Experimenting High Schools.*[1]

Positive Experiences Reported

Alternative high schools in urban, suburban, and rural settings, which use descriptive evaluations, and performance programs such as Concord (suburban: Wilmington, Delaware) and John Adams (urban: Portland, Oregon), report that graduates applying for colleges and jobs have met no meaningful resistance because of nongraded transcripts. Three Chicago area schools—Chicago Metropolitan High School (Metro), St. Mary's Learning Center, and the Center for Self-Directed Learning (New Trier East) report that the acceptances of their graduates by colleges are quantitatively and qualitatively superior to the acceptances of their counterparts from other schools who have gone through traditionally graded programs. The experience of these schools corresponds to reports from other programs that college admissions officers are looking, not for grades, but for the best qualified students.

These four myths (which some educators will continue to believe in spite of research, logic, and good sense) are just some of the half-truths that perpetuate the traditional grading system. As the clear thinkers begin to see that they can, in fact, lead change, they will use the computer to aid learning, evaluating, and reporting; they will devise evaluations which enhance learning; and they will enrich the growth of students as fully functioning individuals, positively addicted to learning.

[1] Howard Kirschenbaum and James A. Bellanca, editors. *College Guide for Experimenting High Schools.* New York: National Humanistic Education Center, 1973.

Contributors

William J. Bailey is an Associate Professor of
Educational Leadership and the Director of the
Center for Educational Leadership at the University of Delaware, Newark. He has served in
the public schools as a teacher, counselor, principal, and assistant superintendent. During his
career, he has been very active in all phases of
grading reform. Bailey is the author of *Managing
Self-Renewal in Secondary Education* (Educational Technology Publications, 1975).

James A. Bellanca is the Coordinator of the
National Center for Grading/Learning Alternatives, Winnetka, Illinois. He is also a teacher at
New Trier East High School in Winnetka, where
he has developed two experimental alternative
programs. He is the author of *Values and the
Search for Self* and *Please Don't Stamp My Child*
(National Education Association, 1975 and 1976,
respectively).

Keith V. Burba, the Principal of the Elms Elementary School, Flushing, Michigan, has worked as a teacher for four and one-half years and as an elementary principal for six years. In both capacities, he has shown a keen interest in effecting needed grading changes in the educational system.

Arthur W. Combs is a former Professor of Education at the University of Florida, Gainesville. He is widely known as a lecturer and consultant on the topics of teacher education and educational psychology. Combs, a past president of ASCD, is the author of *The Professional Education of Teachers: A Perceptual View of Teacher Preparation* (Allyn and Bacon, Inc., 1974) and other books.

Richard L. Curwin is a Professional Development Specialist at the National Technical Institute for the Deaf, Rochester, New York. He is the author of many books and articles related to humanistic education and improving teaching. His publications include *Discovering Your Teaching Self: Humanistic Approaches to Effective Teaching* (Prentice-Hall, Inc., 1975) and *Developing Individual Values in the Classroom* (Learning Handbooks, 1974).

Patrick J. DeMarte is the Director of Competency-Based Teacher Education at the State University College of Arts and Sciences, Geneseo, New York. He has presented papers and conducted workshops on various educational issues at the local and national levels. His most recently published article, "A Look at Some Exemplary Programs: State University College of Arts and Sciences at Geneseo, New York," appears in *Competency-Based Education: A Process for the Improvement of Education* (Prentice-Hall, Inc., 1976).

Patrick J. Dowling is the Assistant Principal of Brecksville Junior High School in a suburb of Cleveland, Ohio. He has taught grades 7-12 in public schools and has served as Academic Director at Glen Oak High School in Cleveland. Dowling has also lectured to and conducted workshops with teachers and administrators at both elementary and secondary levels on the subject of student evaluations.

Francis B. Evans provides consultative and technical services in planning and evaluation to the State of Wisconsin's Department of Public Instruction. In his previous position as Assistant Professor of Education at the University of Wisconsin at Green Bay, he taught courses on the education of children with minority backgrounds, and on educational research and evaluation. He has also taught Navajo Indian children in the public schools.

Lois Borland Hart is the Coordinator of Field Services with the Program for Educational Opportunity at the University of Michigan, East Lansing. She has held a variety of educational positions including those of master teacher, supervisor of student teachers, middle school administrator, and Co-coordinator of the National Conferences on Grading Alternatives (1973). Her recent work has involved the development and implementation of a "Leadership Training for Women" model.

Donald D. Holt is the Principal of Wilton High School, Wilton, Connecticut. Previously, he served for five years as Principal of John Adams High School in Portland, Oregon. As a teacher at the secondary and university levels, and as a practicing school administrator, he has urged students and teachers to question current grading practices, and has participated in numerous workshops and seminars on grading reform.

Philip L. Hosford, a Professor of Education at New Mexico State University, Las Cruces, is the 1976-77 President of the Association for Supervision and Curriculum Development. His publications include *Algebra for Elementary Teachers* (Harcourt, Brace, and World, 1968) and *An Instructional Theory: A Beginning* (Prentice-Hall, Inc., 1973), as well as numerous articles and several booklets. Hosford's present interests and efforts lie in the general field of instruction—its theories, strategies, and tactics.

Howard Kirschenbaum is the Director of the National Humanistic Education Center, Saratoga Springs, New York. He formerly taught English and history in public and private high schools, as well as group dynamics and educational psychology at Temple University, Philadelphia, Pennsylvania. Kirschenbaum is particularly interested in humanistic education, values clarification, and human relations—topics on which he has lectured throughout the United States and abroad.

Rodney W. Napier is a consultant with the Athyn Group, Philadelphia, Pennsylvania. He was formerly an Associate Professor in the Department of Psychoeducational Processes at Temple University in Philadelphia. Napier is co-author of *Groups: Theory and Experience* (Houghton Mifflin Company, 1973) and *Wad-Ja-Get? The Grading Game in American Education* (Hart Publishing Company, 1971).

Sandra Folzer Napier is an Assistant Professor in the Mental Health/Social Service Department at the Community College of Philadelphia, Pennsylvania. She is also a consultant to various institutions and agencies, including National Training Laboratories, the Department of Institutions and Agencies for the State of New Jersey, and others.

Sidney B. Simon is a Professor of Humanistic Education at the University of Massachusetts, Amherst. He is the co-author of *Values Clarification: A Handbook of Practical Strategies for Teachers and Students* (Hart Publishing Company, Inc., 1972) and *Readings in Values Clarification* (Winston Press, 1973), plus other books. Simon—who conducts workshops in values clarification and personal growth in the United States, Canada, and Europe—is presently developing a new theory of human growth.

James B. Van Hoven is the Assistant Superintendent for Instruction, Wilton Public Schools, Wilton, Connecticut. He has been a middle school assistant principal in Chappaqua, New York; a middle school principal in Briarcliff Manor, New York; and a teacher of social studies in Brookline, Massachusetts, and in Stamford, Connecticut.

The National Center for Grading/Learning Alternatives (NCGLA) is a nonprofit educational problem-solving agency.

NCGLA operates on the premise that meaningful solutions to educational problems are best devised through the mutual efforts of teachers, parents, administrators, students, and the local community.

NCGLA conducts in-service training programs to help school and community leaders develop and improve problem-solving skills, provides consultant services in crisis situations, and trains teachers and administrators to create programs that are based on local needs.

NCGLA consultants have special expertise in the areas of competency and effectiveness evaluation of teachers, administrators, and students; alternative learning programs; values clarification; creative problem solving; effectiveness training; positive approaches to discipline; and process skill training. They have worked with school districts to solve problems of vandalism, integration, sex and racial discrimination, and staff redistribution.

For information about NCGLA, write: National Center for Grading/Learning Alternatives, 811 Foxdale, Winnetka, Illinois 60093.

ASCD Publications, Autumn 1976

Yearbooks

Balance in the Curriculum (610-17274)	$5.00
Education for an Open Society (610-74012)	$8.00
Education for Peace: Focus on Mankind (610-17946)	$7.50
Evaluation as Feedback and Guide (610-17700)	$6.50
Freedom, Bureaucracy, & Schooling (610-17508)	$6.50
Leadership for Improving Instruction (610-17454)	$4.00
Learning and Mental Health in the School (610-17674)	$5.00
Life Skills in School and Society (610-17786)	$5.50
A New Look at Progressive Education (610-17812)	$8.00
Perspectives on Curriculum Development 1776-1976 (610-76078)	$9.50
Schools in Search of Meaning (610-75044)	$8.50
Perceiving, Behaving, Becoming: A New Focus for Education (610-17278)	$5.00
To Nurture Humaneness: Commitment for the '70's (610-17810)	$6.00

Books and Booklets

Action Learning: Student Community Service Projects (611-74018)	$2.50
Adventuring, Mastering, Associating: New Strategies for Teaching Children (611-76080)	$5.00
Beyond Jencks: The Myth of Equal Schooling (611-17928)	$2.00
The Changing Curriculum: Mathematics (611-17724)	$2.00
Criteria for Theories of Instruction (611-17756)	$2.00
Curricular Concerns in a Revolutionary Era (611-17852)	$6.00
Curriculum Change: Direction and Process (611-17698)	$2.00
Curriculum Leaders: Improving Their Influence (611-76084)	$4.00
Curriculum Materials 1974 (611-74014)	$2.00
Degrading the Grading Myths: A Primer of Alternatives to Grades and Marks (611-76082)	$6.00
Differentiated Staffing (611-17924)	$3.50
Discipline for Today's Children and Youth (611-17314)	$1.50
Early Childhood Education Today (611-17766)	$2.00
Educational Accountability: Beyond Behavioral Objectives (611-17856)	$2.50
Elementary School Mathematics: A Guide to Current Research (611-75056)	$5.00
Elementary School Science: A Guide to Current Research (611-17726)	$2.25
Eliminating Ethnic Bias in Instructional Materials: Comment and Bibliography (611-74020)	$3.25

Emerging Moral Dimensions in Society: Implications for Schooling (611-75052)	$3.?
Ethnic Modification of Curriculum (611-17832)	$1.?
The Humanities and the Curriculum (611-17708)	$2.?
Humanizing the Secondary School (611-17780)	$2.7?
Impact of Decentralization on Curriculum: Selected Viewpoints (611-75050)	$3.7?
Improving Educational Assessment & An Inventory of Measures of Affective Behavior (611-17804)	$4.5?
International Dimension of Education (611-17816)	$2.2?
Interpreting Language Arts Research for the Teacher (611-17846)	$4.0?
Learning More About Learning (611-17310)	$2.0?
Linguistics and the Classroom Teacher (611-17720)	$2.7?
A Man for Tomorrow's World (611-17838)	$2.2?
Middle School in the Making (611-74024)	$5.0?
The Middle School We Need (611-75060)	$2.5?
Needs Assessment: A Focus for Curriculum Development (611-75048)	$4.0?
Observational Methods in the Classroom (611-17948)	$3.5?
Open Education: Critique and Assessment (611-75054)	$4.7?
Open Schools for Children (611-17916)	$3.7?
Personalized Supervision (611-17680)	$1.7?
Professional Supervision for Professional Teachers (611-75046)	$4.5?
Removing Barriers to Humaneness in the High School (611-17848)	$2.5?
Reschooling Society: A Conceptual Model (611-17950)	$2.0?
The School of the Future—NOW (611-17920)	$3.7?
Schools Become Accountable: A PACT Approach (611-74016)	$3.5?
Social Studies for the Evolving Individual (611-17952)	$3.0?
Strategy for Curriculum Change (611-17666)	$2.0?
Supervision: Emerging Profession (611-17796)	$5.0?
Supervision in a New Key (611-17926)	$2.5?
Supervision: Perspectives and Propositions (611-17732)	$2.0?
The Unstudied Curriculum: Its Impact on Children (611-17820)	$2.7?
What Are the Sources of the Curriculum? (611-17522)	$1.5?
Vitalizing the High School (611-74026)	$3.5?
Developmental Characteristics of Children and Youth (wall chart) (611-75058)	$2.0?

Discounts on quantity orders of same title to single address: 10-49 copies, 10%; 50 or more copies 15%. Make checks or money orders payable to ASCD. Orders totaling $10.00 or less must be prepaid. Orders from institutions and businesses must be on official purchase order form. Shipping and handling charges will be added to billed purchase orders. **Please be sure to list the stock number of each publication, shown in parentheses.**

Subscription to **Educational Leadership**—$10.00 a year. ASCD Membership dues: Regular (subscription and yearbook)—$25.00 a year; Comprehensive (includes subscription and yearbook plus other books and booklets distributed during period of membership)—$35.00 a year.

Order from: **Association for Supervision and Curriculum Development Suite 1100, 1701 K Street, N.W., Washington, D.C. 20006**